BEST RADIO
PLAYS OF 1987

Pearl by John Arden (Special Award 1978)

Best Radio Plays of 1978
Richard Harris: *Is It Something I Said?*
Don Haworth: *Episode on a Thursday
    Evening*
Jill Hyem: *Remember Me*
Tom Mallin: *Halt! Who Goes There?*
Jennifer Phillips: *Daughters of Men*
Fay Weldon: *Polaris*

Best Radio Plays of 1979
Shirley Gee: *Typhoid Mary*
Carey Harrison: *I Never Killed My German*
Barrie Keeffe: *Heaven Scent*
John Kirkmorris: *Coxcomb*
John Peacock: *Attard in Retirement*
Olwen Wymark: *The Child*

Best Radio Plays of 1980
Stewart Parker: *The Kamikaze
    Groundstaff Reunion Dinner*
Martyn Read: *Waving to a Train*
Peter Redgrove: *Martyr of the Hives*
William Trevor: *Beyond the Pale*

Best Radio Plays of 1981
Peter Barnes: *The Jumping Mimuses
    of Byzantium*
Don Haworth: *Talk of Love and War*
Harold Pinter: *Family Voices*
David Pownall: *Beef*
J.P. Rooney: *The Dead Image*
Paul Thain: *The Biggest Sandcastle
    in the World*

Best Radio Plays of 1982
Rhys Adrian: *Watching the Plays Together*
John Arden: *The Old Man Sleeps Alone*
Harry Barton: *Hoopoe Day*
Donald Chapman: *Invisible Writing*
Tom Stoppard: *The Dog It Was That Died*
William Trevor: *Autumn Sunshine*

Best Radio Plays of 1983
Wally K. Daly: *Time Slip*
Shirley Gee: *Never In My Lifetime*
Gerry Jones: *The Angels They Grow Lonely*
Steve May: *No Exceptions*
Martyn Read: *Scouting for Boys*

Best Radio Plays of 1984
Stephen Dunstone: *Who Is Sylvia?*
Robert Ferguson: *Transfigured Night*
Don Haworth: *Daybreak*
Caryl Phillips: *The Wasted Years*
Christopher Russell: *Swimmer*
Rose Tremain: *Temporary Shelter*

Best Radio Plays of 1985
Rhys Adrian: *Outpatient*
Barry Collins: *King Canute*
Martin Crimp: *Three Attempted Acts*
David Pownall: *Ploughboy Monday*
James Saunders: *Menocchio*
Michael Wall: *Hiroshima: The Movie*

Best Radio Plays of 1986
Robert Ferguson: *Dreams, Secrets,
    Beautiful Lies*
Christina Reid: *The Last of a Dyin' Race*
Andrew Rissik: *A Man Alone: Anthony*
Ken Whitmore: *The Gingerbread House*
Valerie Windsor: *Myths and Legacies*

BEST RADIO PLAYS OF 1987

The Giles Cooper Award Winners

Wally K. Daly: Mary's
Frank Dunne: Dreams of Dublin Bay
Anna Fox: Nobby's Day
Nigel D. Moffatt: Lifetime
Richard Nelson: Languages Spoken Here
Peter Tinniswood: The Village Fête

METHUEN/BBC PUBLICATIONS

First published in Great Britain in 1988 by Methuen London,
11 New Fetter Lane, London EC4P 4EE and BBC Publications,
35 Marylebone High Street, London W1M 4AA.

Phototypeset in 9pt Garamond by
Words & Pictures Ltd, Thornton Heath, Surrey

Printed and bound in Great Britain
by Redwood Burn Ltd, Trowbridge, Wiltshire

British Library Cataloguing in Publication Data

Best radio plays of 1987: The Giles Cooper
  Award winners.
  1. Radio plays in English 1945-
  Anthologies
  822'.02'08

  ISBN 0-413-18460-9

CONTENTS

THE GILES COOPER AWARDS: a note on the selection

Giles Cooper

As one of the most original and inventive radio playwrights of the post-war years, Giles Cooper was the author who came most clearly to mind when the BBC and Methuen were in search of a name when first setting up their jointly sponsored radio drama awards in 1978. Particularly so, as the aim of the awards is precisely to encourage original radio writing by both new and established authors – encouragement in the form of both public acclaim and of publication of their work in book form.

Eligibility

Eligible for the awards was every original radio play first broadcast by the BBC domestic service from December 1986 to December 1987 (almost 500 plays in total). Excluded from consideration were translations, adaptations and dramatised 'features'. In order to ensure that the broad range of radio playwriting was represented, the judges aimed to select plays which offered a variety of length, subject matter and technique by authors with differing experience of writing for radio.

Selection

The editors-in-charge and producers of the various drama 'slots' were each asked to put forward about five or six plays for the judges' consideration. This resulted in a 'short-list' of some 30 plays from which the final selection was made. The judges were entitled to nominate further plays for consideration provided they were eligible. Selection was made on the strength of the script rather than of the production, since it was felt that the awards were primarily for writing and that production could unduly enhance or detract from the merits of the original script.

Judges

The judges for the 1987 awards were:
Nicholas Hern, Drama Editor, Methuen London
Richard Imison, Script Editor, BBC Radio Drama
Gillian Reynolds, broadcaster and drama critic of the *Daily Telegraph*
B.A. Young, who was formerly the *Financial Times* drama critic, and who now writes on radio for the same paper

PREFACE

Hyperbole and Hollywood

This is now the tenth volume of "Best Radio Plays" and therefore –
conventionally but in this instance also in fact – something of a
landmark. Fifty-seven published plays would constitute a substantial
body of work in any context; when the authors of those plays
include emergent talents side by side with some of the most
numinous figures in contemporary dramatic writing, and when the
range of style and structure and subject matter is as wide as it has
been over the past ten years, I think we can justifiably regard the
venture as celebrating not just the survival, but the flourishing, of an
art form.

Taken on their own, the statistics of radio drama as an active part
of British cultural life between 1978 and 1988 are really rather
impressive. Leaving aside the wide variety of stage and screenplays,
and the adaptations of novels and stories which are regularly
included in the drama schedule, but which are not eligible for the
Giles Cooper Awards, our fifty-seven winning scripts were chosen by
different panels of judges from some three-and-a-half thousand
original radio plays broadcast by the B.B.C. in those ten years. These
plays had in turn been selected for the most part from among the
hundred thousand completed scripts and synopses submitted to the
Radio Drama department during this period. More than five
thousand writers were regularly involved in writing radio plays – and
very many more occasionally gave the medium a try. All these
figures are dwarfed, however, by that representing the number of
times individual listeners switched on to a radio play in the course of
the past ten years: a prodigious seven billion.

There is a paradox in these figures, in that on the one hand they
seem to belong to the world of Hollywood and hyperbole: the
greatest, the biggest, the most numerous and so forth (and as a
matter of fact it is true that B.B.C. Radio Drama is the largest single
patron of original playwrights in the world). On the other hand we
know that the figures relate to an activity so everyday, and often so
little remarked, as to be in danger of being regarded as commonplace.

As I write, the radio critic of one Sunday newspaper has found a
link between five of last week's plays which has enabled her to
contrast their individual ambitions and degrees of achievement and
at the same time implicitly to recognise that a broad diet of drama is
a natural weekly expectation. As it happens, there were six other
single plays in that week – not to mention a range of serials and
features that in all but an arbitrary classification of provenance and
programme slot could not unreasonably be called plays too. The

choice was both generous and attractive but it is highly unlikely that more than a very small handful of listeners sampled it all.

Indeed, audience research has shown us that the really committed radio drama listener – someone who makes a point of listening as many as five or six times a week – forms a percentage of the audience measured only in single figures. A much more common pattern, even among regular listeners, is that of someone who tunes in only once a week, or even once a fortnight; and of course a proportion of every audience is made up of people who listen a great deal less than that. So the vast patronage figures which relate to radio drama as a whole arise from a pattern of listening throughout society which is decidedly eclectic. We may all have been counted amongst that seven billion but the figure astonishes us because our experience was essentially a personal, individual one, carrying little sense of being shared by others. On Cup Final day at Wembley we can, exceptionally, see in one place a crowd of people equal only to about one fifth of the audience for any Afternoon Play yet the notion seems unreal even in terms of this simple comparison.

The fact is that the radio play is the most democratically available of all dramatic experiences. The technical means of receiving the broadcast signal are inexpensive and universally available; the service itself is free. It is not denied to the elderly, to the disabled or to the blind. It is, increasingly, practically available to those who are travelling or working out of doors. With the advent of the small portable radio with headphones it can remain a personal experience even in a public place. Above all, it is unique among forms of drama in that it can be interpreted broadly according to the taste and experience of the individual listener. In essence, each person hearing a radio play is taking part in something as private as reading a book and their response to it will be even more subjective.

Which leads me to reflect that although this individuality of experience and response is perhaps the most attractive single factor in a medium which has fascinated me for over twenty-five years, it is also what has made the selection of the Giles Cooper plays such a difficult matter – in this volume no less than in the previous nine. Judges' discussions remain confidential and rightly so; to judge anything fairly requires not only skill but a degree of self honesty and willingness to expose one's own fallibility that should not be reported out of context. In these particular awards, however, it has often been the case that a judge's experience of a play has been so intensely satisfying that it has moved in their mind into a dimension which even the author might not have recognised. It has certainly led to some fascinating discussion over the years; it has contributed to some unexpected, even controversial, decisions; ultimately, however, I think it has properly reflected the true condition of radio drama – that it reaches its final form in the imagination of the listener, and not before.

In every volume, the judges have been faced with the dilemma that finding 'best' plays has not always meant comparing like with like. Only the first volume, covering the plays of 1978, formally declared a policy of covering each of the major areas of the B.B.C.'s radio drama output. Thereafter, although the idea of covering different lengths and *genres* of plays has always been considered in the discussions, the final shortlist has always contained the scripts which commanded the greatest support, irrespective of their place in the output. It has meant that narrative thrillers have had to face up to monologues; historical dramas to poetic fantasy; complex aural compositions to pieces in which the only manifestation of radio technique was in the precise use of the word. Time and again it has given rise to a discussion of just what exactly constitutes a good radio play anyway.

When I wrote the first of these prefaces in 1982 (the first three volumes had no introduction beyond a description of the aims and operation of the Awards) I spoke of the radio play as 'a curious beast' in reference to the infinite variety of forms and of subject matter which it can represent. I was immediately taken to task by a critic who, though not unfriendly to the premise of radio drama as an art form, thought that there were really not enough 'curious beasts' to be found. She was right. There weren't. There still aren't. The works that explore and extend any medium, that bring to the spectator or reader or listener that special sense of excitement and revelation that is born of unique perception and meticulous craft, are rare indeed. So the work that is a pure radio play, a wholly aural experience that could not be expressed in any other form is very seldom achieved; often not even attempted.

Yet the development of the radio play over the past ten years has been quite extraordinary on several fronts and it has stemmed not only from the myriad writers, editors, producers, actors and technical staff who created the initial stimulus but also from the much greater number of listeners – frequent or occasional – who form the society that radio drama serves.

That society is currently going through a period of revolution – political, social and technological – which is arguably as fundamental as the Industrial Revolution through which it was passing two hundred years ago. When Wordsworth and Shelley wrote in defence of poetry in the early years of the nineteenth century, they were arguing for humanity and imagination, for philosophy and morality in an age that seemed over-dedicated to the pursuit of material success. 'Poetry', wrote Shelley, 'and the Principle of Self, of which Money is the visible incarnation, are the God and Mammon of the world'.

In our present century, that concept of poetry has become the wider concern of the arts in general and the broadcast arts in particular. What is so readily available to all can be a powerful force for good or it can seem to confirm the least admirable attitudes of pure materialism. It is perhaps the most important of the Reithian tenets of broadcasting that it should entertain, but true entertainment widens horizons on the way.

In this context, radio drama has become a valiant opener of doors – to the past and to literary traditions; to verse and the poetic imagination; to moral and political debate; above all, perhaps, to the experience of other people whose temperament, views or social conditions we do not share. In its multiplicity it can, and does, cover the most catholic range of experiences; in its intimacy it draws the listener into the closest possible identification even with the unfamiliar. The six plays in this volume offer examples of that duality.

By the time this preface is published, at least a hundred more plays will have been broadcast, and a number of new developments embarked upon – of which I should like to mention two. During 1988, the first scheme specifically devoted to discovering and broadcasting the work of young playwrights will be completed: a deliberate investment in the future. And in collaboration with some of the most outstanding members of the film community in Los Angeles, who recognize the relevance to their own medium of the enduring properties of story telling which radio embodies, the B.B.C. will have produced two plays for the first time from the sound stage of a Hollywood film studio. No hyperbole.

Richard Imison
(February 1988)

MARY'S

by Wally K. Daly

For R.I.

Wally K. Daly is the present Deputy Chair of the Writers' Guild of
Great Britain. He has written for every existing length of radio
drama slot, and has had twenty-four half-hour sit-coms broadcast on
Radio 4. He also writes extensively for television. January 1, 1988,
saw the transmission of the TV adaptation of his Giles Cooper
award-winning radio play *Time Slip* – under the new title of *The Giftie*
– and he continues working for the series *Casualty*. His children's
stage musical *Follow the Star* (with music by Jim Parker) continued
its slow circumnavigation of the world with a 1986/87 production
in Bermuda. His most recent radio plays are *Without Fire*, *A Plague
of Goodness* and *Happy Ever After*, all broadcast in 1986 and 1987,
and all polished, improved and produced by Martin Jenkins, Senior
Director, Drama, Radio. *Mary's* came to be written after a challenge
from the actress Elizabeth Rider to attempt to write decent parts
for women; a challenge for which the author is now duly grateful.
He is also grateful to those who, in spite of the play's controversial
nature, fought gamely over a four-year period to have it recorded
and broadcast.

Mary's was first broadcast on BBC Radio 3 on 13 October 1987. The cast was as follows:

MARY, *mother of Jesus*   Barbara Jefford
MARY MAGDALENE   Imelda Staunton

Director: Martin Jenkins
Running time, as broadcast: 58 minutes, 26 seconds

Time: two days after Jesus' crucifixion. Dusk.
Place: outside the tomb.

Sound effects: three knocks representing the nails being hammered into Jesus' hands/feet; a loud, long clap of robust thunder; pouring rain dissolving into the stone being rolled across the front of the tomb, followed by low, sustained wind with occasional, distant thunder throughout the play.

MARY. He's dead. He really is dead. And soon . . . he will rise again. Finally it will be confirmed that I spoke the truth. He *is* the son of God. The stories will start to spread even further. Small truths will grow into bigger truths. Little lies will grow into bigger lies. And in his . . . resurrection, he shall live forever. As will his mother.

That woman from Magdalene is an irritation. She'll spoil everything if she goes on like this. 'He's not really dead!' 'He doesn't need to rise again – he's still among us!' She knows how important it is that he *is* dead. And that he will rise again. She's only trying to . . . irritate me.

I had her marked out from the start. I watched her antics. Making moon eyes at him. I knew her game. Even went so far as to kneel in front of him and wash his feet. I knew what she was up to. The front of her dress hanging forward, loose – her head thrown back so that . . . Yes – I knew what she was up to all right. Didn't do her any good. Not with my boy. He knew he was meant for greater things. Wasn't swayed from his path by the call of the flesh.

MAGDALENE. The mother killed him. As assuredly as if she'd hammered in the nails or stuck the spear in his side she killed him. But they tell me to 'Keep quiet about it'. 'Don't spoil everything.' Keep quiet? Don't spoil everything? Oh no. I won't keep quiet. I'll shout my story 'til it echoes from the sky. The whole world shall know that that mockery of a woman murdered

him as assuredly as if she'd stuck a knife in him. Always goading
him on. Always shoving destiny down his throat. 'You know what
you were born to do.' 'You know what is written in the book.'
Now they want me to keep quiet. Well I won't. I won't just stand
by mute and let them do this to his memory. They're setting out
to turn him into some sort of freakish God. He was just a man.
A very special man; with a very special message. But just a man.
A man who sweated in the heat. Smelt a bit. Who hawked and
spat when the dust clogged his throat, the same as anyone does.

A man who felt the heat between his legs even though he
fought against it; a man who scratched when he itched, no matter
where he itched. The way they're starting to paint him now
he didn't even need to relieve himself. They're trying to turn
him into some sort of temple statue. A dead thing without
feeling. No heart, no love. He wasn't like that . . . He wasn't like
her . . . He was alive – he was real. And now he's dead . . . And she
murdered him.

MARY. Apparently she's saying I murdered him. Silly woman. Also
says that, if he doesn't rise again – if the prophecy isn't fulfilled, it
would confirm that I'd been lying from the very start. Right from
the very moment of his conception. How could I lie about a thing
like that? The most perfect night of my life.

The quality of a dream. But it was real. I lay in my bed alone –
as always. The shutters open. No breeze to turn over the air to a
cooler side. I could feel my own heat – tacky – and lay happy in
my heat, dreaming young girl dreams of Joseph, so near but not
yet mine. Wondering, as all young girls must have sometimes
wondered, what it would be like . . .

. . . And then I knew I was no longer alone. No door had
opened. The window was in my view. No one had entered – but
I was no longer alone. 'Be not afraid.' The voice, a velvet whisper
in my mind bolted me in my bed – set a pulse racing in my neck.
And I saw him at the foot. Saw him – then didn't see him. He
hazed somewhere between this world and that.

And I knew it wasn't a man. This golden presence shaped as
man was much, much more than man. 'Who are you?' No reply.
Simply a smile. 'Be not afraid,' he said. And with that smile there
was no more fear.

When he saw that – he . . . moved over me; wrapped me
around; a weightless golden being who blotted out the night.
I wanted to cry out 'It's wrong. I'm betrothed. I mustn't be with
child.' But no words came. I simply opened to him. And felt him,
knowing the moment was right, melt into every part of my being.
And then he was gone. Nine months later my son was born.

MAGDALENE. How the neighbours must have laughed when she
told them. 'An Angel, Mary? How lovely for you. Did he have a
big one, like? Or a little one? Of course you wouldn't know,

would you, Mary? Being a good Jewish girl, and not having
anything to compare it with, like.' I can imagine the women
outside their houses, sniggering together. Pointing her out to
other women in the market place. Giggling. Always giggling.
Serve her *right*. She had her fun. Only *right* that she should
pay for it.

Poor old Joseph. How much nudging and winking did he have
to put up with as well? Especially after he told them he'd also
been visited by an Angel, who confirmed that she'd spoken the
truth. 'You also had a visit, Joseph? That's nice. What chances of
you getting pregnant as well then?' Perhaps he just stayed inside
the shop. That's the answer when Angels come to visit – leaving
pregnant women behind them – stay in the shop and keep away
from your neighbours. Not that I disbelieve her, mind. Oh, no.
I believe her. We've all been visited by Angels at some time in our
lives, haven't we? And come to that, many a little devil's been
inside as well. I remember – just after the first time I had the
bleeding – I'd just turned eleven – started quite young – my
mother said I had Granny's blood in me. A wild one, Granny was.
When she was young she ran away – unheard of. Left her children
without a mother for two years. Then one day she came back –
just like that. Unchanged, apparently – except for her eyes. My
mother said they were like 'pools of pain'. Reckoned she couldn't
look into them without wanting to cry. Anyway – after the initial
joy of her return, my grandfather, naturally, beat her – asking her
where she'd been.

She never told him. She never told anyone.

She refused to speak of it all her life. Except – when she was
dying, she said, 'I'm glad I went. It was worth the beating.' Then
she died. Grandad was furious. So there I was. Eleven years old –
Granny's blood inside me – and ready for anything. Not really
sure what the anything was.

I finally learnt what it was at Granny's funeral. There was a lot
of relatives staying with us for the occasion. And when it was
growing late I was sent off to sleep in the storage space above the
main room. It was windowless and airless, and almost pitch black.
Too hot for any covering and no one to see me in the dark.

So I lay there and listened. I could hear all the family singing
and talking outside. It was a very warm and friendly sound.
I felt comforted and unafraid. I lay for a long while unable to
sleep, but finally – I was just dozing off, lulled by the noise
outside, when I heard a step on the ladder leaning against the
storage place where I lay. I heard a rung creak. Then another step
and another creak. And I realised that someone was slowly
coming up the ladder to where I lay naked. 'Who is it?'
I whispered. There was no reply. Within seconds a figure was
beside me. Too dark to see who it was. I couldn't even make out
if it was a man or a woman. But I wasn't afraid.

My family was so near outside that, if I'd cried out, they would have been at my side in seconds. So I wasn't afraid. Just excited at the adventure – Granny's blood, you see. 'Who is it?' I whispered for the second time. 'Don't be afraid,' the figure whispered back. Then, in a voice full of . . . oratory – whispered oratory, that is –he said, 'I am about to give you a gift from God'. 'Really?' I said. 'Oh, yes!' he replied. 'I have to put it in a special place that God has made for it.'

'It may hurt a little at first – and just in case it does hurt – before I put the present in the special place – I'll cover your mouth with my hand for a few seconds.'

But there was no pain. Not that first time.

Oh yes – he was an Angel all right. And he brought me a present from God every night for a whole week. Until they went away that is.

MARY. It was a difficult time for Joseph. He had to put up with a lot of cruel mockery from the other men. He became very short with me, even after he'd had the dream that confirmed I'd spoken the truth. It seemed as though there was still a seed of doubt.

The funny thing about his dream was that I didn't ever really believe it had happened. It just seemed too convenient. Too good to be true. I mean, it didn't stop the neighbours talking – well, a whole flock of Angels in the village square wouldn't have done that – but it made them slightly more careful about saying anything directly to us, just in case what we'd both said *was* true, and that God might take vengeance on them on our behalf. And the children stopped calling those awful names after me in the street and throwing the pebbles.

Funny, really. I was furious with him when he doubted my story – screamed at him, 'How dare you suggest that I would lie about something like that? How dare you doubt my word, you evil old man?'

Then – days later – he had his dream; and I doubted him. Something in his eyes suggested he was lying. Just comforting me. It seemed best that I went away for a while. So I did. I went through the mountains to visit my cousin Elizabeth.

It was extraordinary; when I got there, I discovered that *she* was pregnant as well, and that Zacharias, her husband, had been struck dumb and the reason why – for doubting her! And only then did I start to believe that Joseph might have spoken the truth about his dream.

MAGDALENE. 'Just baby fat,' my mother would say. 'Just baby fat.' And my father would 'Umph' – a sound somewhere between hopefulness and disbelief – and then go about his business, tending to the olives or whatever. As for Mother, I think she knew from the very first month.

By the fourth month there was no denying it. My belly was

pumpkin tight. My breasts swelled like water melons; the nipples standing permanently erect, pushing hard through the cloth.
I tried to keep out of Father's way as much as possible. Almost didn't see him for weeks at a time. But I knew there was a reckoning coming. And so did Mother. Her fears of Granny's blood had been confirmed. She was obviously crying a lot – her eyes rimmed red, her face suddenly very old, very tired.

She spent her days hoping against hope that she was wrong. But knowing in her heart, and in her head, that she wasn't. Finally, the reckoning came.

I came into the meal late. My brothers, sisters, Mother, Father all sat eating, talking happily. I walked in through the door, silhouetted against the sunlight, and turned to go to my place in the dark of the corner.

'Stop!' Father's cry transfixed me. I didn't dare move. I stood, knowing my belly was etched against the sunlight. The room was absolutely hushed. It seemed as if the whole village had gone quiet. I heard my father rising from his place, coming towards me, and I didn't dare to turn and face him. I simply looked at the floor. There was a long pause as he viewed my new strange shape. Then he cupped my chin with one of those gigantic hands of his – and he jerked my head up and round roughly, so that I faced him. He'd stooped so his face was within inches of mine. His eyes burned into me. And the words cracked out through the tension in his throat almost as a whisper, 'Who did this thing to you?'

I knew by then that it had been Uncle Jerome who visited me on the shelf – the nicest of my uncles, I decided. The last night of the visit I'd made a point of finding out. But I also knew that Father, and my elder brother, would kill him, or at least remove his manhood, if they knew who it was. And I couldn't let that happen, not to Uncle Jerome, he was too nice for that – but who else could I blame?

So I answered. Quite cheerily. 'God's representative visited me – said he had a present.'

I saw the fist coming at me. I could see the little hairs on the front of each knuckle, see that the knuckles looked like large, hard knobs of wood on a thick and brittle branch, each tip white with the tension of the fist he'd made, the thumb tucked in, tight, also white with tension. And then it landed full in my face. He'd never struck me in his life 'til that moment.

I felt my nose crumbling under the impact, felt my lips being pushed in, on to, and through, my teeth. Felt teeth snapping from gums, my mouth instantly filling with gouts of blood. And then I was flying.

Flying to a corner, lifted bodily by the power of the blow, but feeling no pain – or feeling too much pain to comprehend – then landing and bowling over Mother and my little sister, Anna, who sat where I fell, scattering their food.

Vaguely, in the nightmare of my flight, I heard my father scream . . . 'Sacrilegious whore!' . . . 'Sacrilegious whore!' . . . They were the last words he ever spoke to me.

MARY. When I discovered Joseph hadn't arranged anywhere for us to stay in Bethlehem, I was more furious than I've ever been about anything in my life.

So many family and friends, so many possible places, and he hadn't arranged anywhere for us to stay. We were very distant with each other by that time in any case. It hadn't been an easy pregnancy. I was being sick right up to the very last month. And the heat made my belly itch intolerably, and he hated to see me scratching it. Didn't understand the need.

We'd also been having . . . discussions . . . about how we would register the baby, if it was born before the day of census. If it went under Joseph's name, a child of the House of David, it would be a lie, as it wasn't his child; it was God's. 'So what am I supposed to do?' he said. 'Write down "A Son of God"?' 'Yes,' I said, 'Write that down – he *is* the Son of God!'

Finally it was decided – we would leave the decision to God. We hoped it would be born after we'd returned home – then it wouldn't need to be registered at all, but, if it wasn't, it was to be registered as a child of the House of David. It would be God's decision which it was to be.

The journey was a nightmare; seemed to last forever. And the resting place we finally found when we got there was a hovel. Not even a shed. Just a ramshackle lean-to at the side of a tumble-down house. You could see the starlight through gaps in the planks of wood, and it stank to high heaven. It seemed the animals there hadn't been cleaned out for weeks. The floor strewn with filthy straw, droppings everywhere, and nowhere else but the floor to sit.

Soon after arriving there, my waters broke. That didn't help. I think I probably brought it on early by sobbing so much – the exhaustion, the sheer awfulness of it all finally being too much for me – I was sobbing. And then I felt it coming. Joseph went to try to find somebody to help, trying unsuccessfully to hide his panic. When he'd gone I lifted up my skirts and squatted, waiting. Then the agony began. I was being ripped apart and still it wouldn't come. Didn't want to come. It seemed as though little fingers had dug into the walls of the womb and wouldn't let go.

I screamed with the pain, lost my bowels and had to move, but still it wouldn't come. I thought I would die. And my screams grew so loud I thought my head would split.

The animals bellowed and pawed the ground and kicked out the planking with terror. Suddenly kind hands were helping. Joseph had found an old woman. There was blood everywhere.

But the child was finally born.

There was no water of course, so the old lady spat on a piece of
rag and wiped its eyes and nose clean, then gave him to me where
I lay, totally drained, on the filthy straw.

He was beautiful. So beautiful.

People were by now crowding into the lean-to. My screams had
made everyone fear that there was a murder afoot, and they
dashed to check what was happening. So many people that there
was hardly room to move – but I didn't care. They crushed in to
wonder at the beauty of this baby born in a barn, jostling each
other to get a better view; men in incredible finery mingling
shoulder to shoulder with simple shepherds, all eager to see
my son.

And only Joseph and I knew that – the Son of God had finally
been born – as promised.

MAGDALENE. The old woman that Father made Mother take me
to was somewhere between a witch and a sort of doctor. She lived
in a hovel in a clearing in the forest. Nobody ever went there
unless they had needs.

My father had needs. If he couldn't kill this person who had
defiled his property, he could at least rip out his spawn. I didn't
count, of course. It wasn't even discussed with me. I was an
object. An object getting between Father and his vengeance.

So Mother was made to take me to the old crone, money
clutched hot in her hand.

I wasn't frightened of her. It stood to reason that if she could
really perform magic, make spells that worked, she'd have sorted
herself out long ago; got rid of the bend in her back; straightened
out the twisted shoulder perhaps. Certainly she'd have at least
sorted out her face – the moles and the hair. But no – there she
was, standing in the doorway in the sunlight, as ugly and wrinkled
as ever, cackling away and wringing her hands with delight
at the money.

No. I wasn't afraid of her. But Mother was. She wouldn't go
inside. Said she'd stay outside and look at the plants.

So I had to go in alone.

Mostly – I remember her hands. I can see them today as clearly
as I can still see Father's, mashing my face. Her's rheumy and
twisted, with dirty claws, rake-long, protruding; rolling her
sleeves high, ready to get on with her evil work.

MARY. The strange thing was that in Egypt we grew together.

You see, his second dream was so clear. He sat bolt upright in
the straw and screamed me awake. He said the Angel had told him
all babies were to be butchered in a three mile area, and had
shown him the slaughter that was to come. As he spoke of his
dream he was quickly putting our bundle together, gathering our
belongings for the journey. Made me get up and dress. I said
I'd go and warn the mothers. You see, at a time like that, when

you stay in a place for a while with a new baby, you get to know the mothers. Meet them at the temple, all proud to show off their babies – same as I showed off mine.

I should imagine there was no more than sixty or seventy of us in the area. Babies whose names I'd been told – and still remember. Lots of Rachels and Annas and Ephriams and Josephs.

No more than a couple of hours' work to warn them all. But Joseph wouldn't let me. He said the warning from the Angel was for us, just for us.

Too many running away would make it unsafe – we'd be caught. Less than a hundred yards away, a baby had been born two nights before – a little girl – and he wouldn't even let me warn her mother. And I swore then I would loathe him for the rest of my life for his heartlessness. But I didn't. In Egypt I started to love him. A little.

We hid on the outskirts, behind a large rock shaded by brushwood and grass. We heard the screaming begin. And then the wailing that followed, that awful wailing. I pictured the butchery in my mind's eye – saw the flash of swords and the thrust of spears through swaddling. Plump bellies split . . . little heads . . .

Just before dawn, the screaming stopped – but the wailing went on and on. It seemed to dog our footsteps for miles and miles and miles.

But in Egypt I saw, finally, that Joseph was indeed a man. And let him know me – as a man – for the very first time.

MAGDALENE. After poking at my belly, weighing my breasts in her hands, deciding how far gone I was, she made me a potion – made me drink it down. Foul. Ugh! I tried to stop half way, but she'd not have that. 'All of it! All of it!' So I drank it all. Within seconds my head was spinning – a really nice sensation. I even started giggling a bit. If I'd known what was coming, perhaps I wouldn't have been quite so happy.

In the middle of it all, while I was lying bathed in sweat, it kicked me. For the very first time my baby kicked me. As if to say, 'Don't worry, Mum. That old witch will have to do better than that to get me out of here.'

And she did.

As darkness fell I heard her go out to Mother. Heard her say I must stay the night as other things were necessary. I was too far gone for the potion. My mother didn't come inside, she just went away without saying a word.

At some point – a prick of pain speared me deep inside.

When she collected me at dawn the next day, I was no longer with child.

Pause.

I vowed my father would pay for what he'd paid her to do.

To let your own daughter be so abused.
Through my tears I vowed he would pay – and he did.

MARY. In Nazareth we led a quiet life. Joseph was a good craftsman,
never short of work. And now we were truly married. The scandal
almost died away. The occasional vicious comment of course, but
nothing like before. And the baby grew.

I let him know from the start that he was special. Taught him to
be wary of childish badness. The games of 'discovery' children
have played with each other since time began were never played
by him. And because of that, because of him being 'special' and a
little distant, they thought him . . . strange. And they did, I admit,
tell lies about him.

When young Tobias died, the other children said it was the way
Jesus had looked at him after losing the game they'd been
playing. Said he'd stared at Tobias in a certain way – and he'd
simply dropped down dead. Silliness. He was just a good boy, and
they were jealous of his goodness. We never had one iota of
trouble throughout his childhood. Never saw any of this
'strangeness'. Which is why, perhaps, it came as such a shock
when he ran away when we were in Jerusalem for the Passover.

Only twelve years old and he ran away. On the way back, when
I realised he'd gone, wasn't with the rest of the family, it seemed
as though my whole being emptied; left a cold void of fear where
fluttered my frightened heart. He'd gone – but where?

And the tongues started lashing again – 'What fine parents
they've turned out to be. Not even knowing their child was
missing for so many days.'

We searched – in desperation we back-tracked over every foot
of our journey from Jerusalem, asking everyone along the way if
they'd seen our son.

And as we went on our way I screamed at Joseph that it was his
fault; that he'd never loved him; always been jealous of him
because of the way I treated him. That he wanted him out of the
way – and that I hoped God would strike him dead in punishment
for his carelessness in losing God's son.

But Joseph never uttered a syllable in reply. Simply went on
searching. It must have been almost more of a relief to Joseph,
when we finally found Jesus in the temple, than it was to me. But
there was worse to follow. I was too relieved to tongue-lash Jesus
strongly for frightening us so much. I left that to Joseph. And
wished I hadn't.

With just a few words Jesus cut him to the heart. 'Don't you
realise I must be about My *Father's* business?' he said. But really
viciously. He was deliberately speaking to hurt. It was as if Joseph
had been slapped across the face. High spots of colour sprang to
his cheek, his mouth so tight he had a white line round his lips.

From that day Joseph was never the same again. It seemed

almost as though he'd shrivelled up inside.

Jesus knew. Without being told, he knew that Joseph wasn't his real father.

MAGDALENE. My vengeance upon my father was sweet. No one was safe from me. 'Whore,' he called me. I proved him right. As promised, I made him pay. But it wasn't only revenge. My belly had been full of baby. Now it was simply an empty vessel that ached to be filled.

Young shepherd boys, merchants passing through and taking water at the well, cousins, business associates of my father, my elder brother, the gardeners in the olive grove. The vessel had to be filled. But it never was. Whatever the old crone had done, she'd done well. I was never to be with child again.

Finally the scandal grew too great. And Father hit upon the perfect solution – he'd marry me off. I felt fairly safe – who would marry such a little tart? – but I shouldn't have been so confident. The old silversmith would.

I can't bring myself to talk about him, even today. Merely to think of that wizened old disaster of a man, even after all these years, makes my stomach heave. Sufficient to say that following in Granny's footsteps seemed infinitely preferable.

So I ran away. First I went to Uncle Jerome's. He was very pleased, and Auntie was quite understanding. Of course I could stay, help her with the children. She was slightly less understanding three months later, the morning she came back from the market early and found me happily bedded with Uncle Jerome.

Within the hour I was back on the road, her screams ringing in my ears. Nowhere to go and no money. Two days later, my thirteenth birthday – so hungry my gut growled – I sold my body for the very first time. And the price? A chunk of bread; a small, stale, dry chunk of bread; and a sip of wine.

MARY. There was no further trouble. He grew to manhood, learnt the trade from Joseph. And, when Joseph grew too old to work, took over the business completely, became a master of the craft. Still kept away from women, which pleased me – he was meant for greater things.

His friends were the other young men of the village. The talk was of crops, of trade, of fishing, of politics, not of women. Never again did he cause us any heartache.

I must admit, he was so placid that I almost began to fear that the Angel had been mistaken, and that that old blind man in the temple had also been mistaken. Where was this sword that would pierce my heart? Was I to die without it being unsheathed?

I confess there is a special pride in knowing one's child is somehow special. And I must also confess that I often asked him if he felt it was time yet, had he felt 'destiny' calling, received any orders from God?

He took it in good part. Always smiled at me with that gentle smile of his and told me to be patient. When the time was right, he'd know it.

That Magdalene whore says I nagged him. That's not true. I was just naturally interested. I wasn't 'goading him', as she says. I wasn't 'ramming destiny down his throat'. I was just – interested.

One day, when he was about thirty, he put down the piece of wood he was shaping and came into the main room, taking his apron off as he entered, and said 'I must go for a walk in the desert – think things over'.

My heart lept with joy. This could perhaps be the start. He pecked me on the forehead, as was his way, and within minutes was striding off through the village without a backward glance. And I was proud. If this was the start, I had done my duty well. I had guided and guarded him as only a Jewish mother knows how. He was going off to face his destiny, unsullied.

MAGDALENE. Every large town had an area where one could practice one's trade in peace. And very soon, with practice, I became a master craftsman, earned a good living.

I never had anyone I didn't like the look of. Always refused to have Romans, which was only proper. Ugly people didn't appeal. So I – almost – enjoyed what I was doing – with my carefully chosen clientele. And when one town palled, I'd simply move on to the next. Except, sometimes, just before dawn, when work had finished for the night, and I drifted near to sleep, my mind would turn to my poor dead baby. And, as in my mind's eye he grew with the passage of the years, I often wondered what he would think of his mother's chosen way of life. No – not chosen – there was no other option if I was to go on living. But what would he think of me? I hoped he would be generous enough to understand.

So, life was good. I was doing to the best of my ability the only thing I could do. Until one day something happened – something that . . . after which, I was never able to feel clean again. Until the first time *he* looked at me, that is.

Once every year, when I was a child, my father used to do business in Tiberius. I'd never quite understood what business it was. But the town itself was a magnet to me. And after two or three years of plying my trade, I ended up there.

For only the second time in my new career I was working with a group of girls – all of them very nice and very young – under a rather fat madam, who was kindness itself.

We had a beautifully decorated salon in which we sat every evening, in the flimsiest and finest of silks, with our faces veiled – Madam insisted on veils. As she said, 'A small mystery always increases the desire'.

And time drifted away happily. Days merged into days and season into season, until finally I hardly knew what time of the year it was. If I had known, perhaps it wouldn't have happened. But it did.

One night, just after we opened for business, three men walked into the salon, slightly the worse for wine, looked at the girls on display, quickly made their choice, and left the salon for the rooms above. I was one of the three chosen.

The one who chose me, hidden behind my veil, was my father.

I left the room with him. Walked up the stairs ahead of him, his hands fondling me greedily from behind, into my room. I walked over to stand in the shaft of light slicing through the window, so he could see me clearly. Then I took my veil off. 'Hello, Father,' I said. His face was full of disbelief.

He stood, mouth agape, staring at the body of this whore before him, pink painted nipples clearly visible through the silk of the gown, as was the crevice to Paradise, combed and parted, ready for the weary traveller; but with the face of Mary, his child, who said simply, 'Hello, Father'. For what seemed like an age he stood silent.

Then he started screaming, his eyes almost popping with the pressure of his screams. Then he turned and fled the room.
I was never to feel clean again . . . until the day *he* looked at me, that is.

MARY. Soon the stories began to filter back. I heard from Elizabeth of his meeting with her son, John – the one people had started calling The Baptist. And together we shared the joy of finally proving the neighbours wrong to have doubted our visits from the Angels all those years before.

And as months progressed the stories grew – the miracles, the loaves and fishes, the walking on water, the lovely sermons he was giving – I knew I would soon have to join him.

Women have been known to be . . . attracted . . . by that sort of power. The Devil has been known to tempt the strongest spirit, as strong as my son's even. I knew I must go to his side, join him, to help protect him.

I tried to explain it to Joseph but his attitude was very strange. It was almost as if he wished it wasn't happening. As if he wished the prophecy'd been proved wrong. That Jesus was just a normal child, grown to be a normal man. I asked him what was the matter, but he wouldn't talk of it.

I mean, I knew he wasn't happy when he had to take up the tools again. I said to him, 'You can't have everything. If we're blessed with a son who's very special, one has to make sacrifices.'

And I swear he muttered grumpily, 'He's no son of mine.'
But he was hammering a chisel with a mallet at the time so I could be wrong.

Still, I knew I must soon join him in his travels. Knew he'd be pleased to see me. Knew he wouldn't mind me spending some days with him. Before he died, that is.

Oh yes, I knew he was destined to die. I knew that that was the sword I would have to bear. Common knowledge that the Saviour to be born must die to save Mankind – but then would rise again. And he was to be the Saviour. But I was surprised how little time he actually had. When the realisation finally struck me, the last time we all had supper together a few days before they crucified him, I remember being totally shocked. And then a strange feeling of relief swept over me.

The Magdalene woman was being very persistent at that time. I'd told him to send her away, but he wouldn't. So, in a funny sort of way, it was a relief – that that worry was soon to be passed.

MAGDALENE. I started travelling from town to town again, always making sure before I settled that there was good water to bathe in.

Bathing had become my favourite occupation. It didn't do any good, of course. Since seeing my father I felt dirty somewhere deep inside where the waters could never reach.

Until one day, bathing in a pool shaded by trees at the very edge of the desert, *he* came upon me naked.

Funny how coy one is about one's body, even when one's using it to earn a living. I'd never strip down at the water until I was sure no one was present.

The day in question, a bake-oven day with the sun a mad red eye in the blue of the sky, no one had been present and I'd stripped and dived, baby-bare, into the cool embrace of the water. Played like a child, twirling and thrashing until – exhausted – I turned on my back and floated. It was then that I saw him.

He was standing where I'd dropped my clothes on the sandy shore. He'd obviously walked over the dunes, out of the desert. And now stood silent with the sun hot behind him. I couldn't see his face, but there was no sense of threat. Only a sense of peace. And I knew this was a good man who watched me and that I had nothing to fear.

Slowly I swam back to the bank, climbed out of the water and walked naked and unashamed to where he stood by my clothes.

I stood in front of him, silent, and, for the first time, I saw his face. And for the first and only time in my life, knew what love was. He was looking at my nakedness. But not in a hungry way. Almost with a sense of wonder. As if I was the first naked woman he'd ever seen.

And I was pleased and proud that my body was so beautiful for him. I could feel my breasts blossoming under his gaze, the nipples hardening under the cool drops of water still glistening on their swell. Without knowing I was going to speak, I spoke.

'Do you want me?' He didn't reply. Just went on viewing my body for what seemed an age. Then he spoke, softly, the only words he said to me that day . . . 'Turn round.' . . .

. . . And I did. And I imagined his eyes viewing me from behind.
My hair, moulded with water, I knew would be lying the whole
length of my back to rest just on the curve of my buttocks.
And with the sense of pleasure of being viewed, they clenched
tight, dimpling before his gaze.

I sensed when he'd seen enough, without being told, and turned
to face him again.

His eyes locked on mine. He didn't give another glance to my
body, just held eyes. Eyes that invited me in. And deep inside
those eyes, I saw the love and warmth and the sheer goodness of
the man. And when he knew I'd seen this, he smiled. A smile fit to
break the heart of the world.

Then he turned and walked back into the sun, over the dunes
and into the desert. I don't know how long I stood and stared
after him. The heat of the day had dried my body and still I stood.
How long I will never know. But I do know that for the first time
since the night in the whorehouse in Tiberius, when my father
had chosen me, I was truly, truly clean. And never, from that day
to this, was I to sell my body again. I was his, and his alone, until
the day I died. And would only ever give myself on his behalf.

MARY. It was a good supper, that last one we had together. But
there was an expectancy in the air. It was as if the heat of the
room was building to a storm. You could feel the explosive
power. The laughter was too forced, the chatter too gay. They
knew it too – you could tell. It was written in their sweating faces,
their shaking hands.

Of course the pressure on the streets and in the town was great,
too. One could see the Romans had nearly had enough; so had
the priests. Both obviously felt threatened by him, but it was
more than that. It was in the room.

Something that would shatter the world asunder and shift the
destiny of man. When it finally came, it seemed such a small
thing, a pin-prick almost, but a large enough pin to prick the
tension as if it were a boil.

I was sorry it had to be Judas. He was a nice boy, in his own
funny way. Always a bit outside the group, as though he was there
more by accident than design, a sort of afterthought. But I liked
him in spite of that. He talked to me a lot over the months when
I visited them. He was a bit lonely I think.

He told me a strange thing once, that troubled me until I saw
its meaning. He said that when he joined the group, and Jesus
kissed him in welcome, as he always did with his new disciples,
that Jesus was laughing, inside his eyes, as if at a secret joke. And
when Judas asked him why he laughed, Jesus told him that he was
the lynch-pin. Without him nothing was possible and, with him,
people's attitude to him, it would be a constant reminder that
Jesus had failed. Judas was to be the one man who would never
find forgiveness in the heart of Mankind.

Love thy neighbour; forgive those who trespass; turn the other
cheek – for Judas none of the basic rules would apply. He would
be universally hated and despised till the end of time, his
name a curse.

And I think, finally, that night of the supper, I had begun to
understand what my son had meant.

After the supper, Judas was waiting in my room crying bitterly.
Said it wasn't true, he would never betray my son, never. So . . . I
explained everything to him . . . What my son had meant about
him being the lynch-pin, what was written, what was necessary.

And finally, some hours later, having decided to pay the high
price asked of him, he went to do – what had to be done.

MAGDALENE. I knew he was to be my life. I went and found him
and his group and travelled with them to the very end. The others
didn't like me. Thought his purity was at risk – wanted to drive
me away. But he wouldn't let them. I think they were only
jealous. Jealous of the special way he looked at me – the few times
he took any notice of me, that is. The way a mother looks at a
new-born child – a caress in each smallest glance.

So I travelled with them, keeping in the background, hiding at
the corner of his life, eating with them but apart. Always there if
he ever wanted me like that. But I came to realise he never would.
And slowly they all began to accept me. Except for the mother.
She never accepted me. And I never trusted her. I always felt she
much preferred the God in him to the son in him. Once Jesus let
me wash his feet in her presence. And I was so happy at being
allowed to touch him, even if only his feet, that, kneeling in front
of him, I flung my head back, my eyes tight closed, and laughed
with the sheer joy of the privilege.

And opened my eyes to see her standing at my shoulder,
looking down at me. Not at my face, but down the front of my
garment. And on her face was a look of loathing and disgust
which I couldn't begin to comprehend.

Jesus never asked me to wash his feet again. I think perhaps
she'd said something to him about it.

So – I never trusted her. Which is why I watched outside her
room that night of the supper, when I saw that Judas had slipped
in. I couldn't hear what was being said through the door. So
I waited at the end of the corridor, hiding in shadow, until he left.

I knew he'd been crying when he went in, had heard his sobs.
But when he came out, his face was so full of resolve, he was so
sure of himself, that it frightened me. And I knew I must find out
what had changed him so.

He didn't want to come with me, said there were other things
he must do. But finally he came back to my room and after a
promise of good wine, told me everything.

If Jesus wasn't betrayed, he would go on preaching, grow old,
die and be forgotten, the same as the thousands of other wise

men who'd gone before him. But if he died now, died for what he believed, then rose again, his memory would live forever. He would be proved to be the Son of God.

Judas said he must betray him. Said that that was what Jesus really wanted him to do. So he could fulfil the prophecy. I told him it was madness, crazy. No man can rise from the dead. Told him that was simply what the mother wanted.

'Ask Jesus,' I said. He wouldn't listen. She'd convinced him too thoroughly. His mind was set. I begged him on my knees to stay. I wanted Jesus to live. Said I'd give him anything if he stayed, anything!

He came back to stand in front of me. His eyes burnt down on me; into me; in a way I'd never seen before.

'You could give only your body,' he said. 'I shall give my life.' Then he smiled. 'Which of us is the luckier?' And I knew what he meant.

Then he went off happily and sold Jesus to the priests for thirty pieces of silver – less than I used to earn on a good night.

I searched for Jesus to warn him. When I finally found them at the Garden of Gethsemane it was too late. The soldiers had arrived at the gate just before I did.

MARY. It was a strangely exciting day. The crowd thronging the square were in holiday mood. They jostled each other and laughed and milled about. Children ran everywhere, pickpockets were having a field day. All the while the sellers cried their wares and the beggars hobbled hopeful.

Suddenly Jesus was brought out on to the balcony by Pontius Pilate and a cheer went up from the crowd. They liked him. I was proud of the way he stood unbowed even though he'd obviously been handled very roughly.

But there was someone else with him on the other side of Pilate. Barabbas.

The crowd booed him strong to show their dislike of this murdering monster. But then a thought crossed my mind. What if the people were to be offered a choice? Jesus or Barabbas? The crowd would call for Jesus to be freed. They hated Barabbas, loathed him.

It mustn't happen. It must not be allowed to happen. He mustn't be freed. It was his destiny to die. But how to stop it . . .

MAGDALENE. When Pilate spoke, saying, 'Either Jesus or Barabbas can go free. Make your choice!' the whole square stilled. Silence fell like a shroud over the throng. It was a joke. A bad taste joke. That *was* no choice. The people hated Barabbas. He was a thief and a murderer. Jesus would go free. Just one cry would start them off and they'd all be screaming their agreement. 'Give us Jesus!'

I saw some Roman soldiers watching me and was afraid to be

the first to shout. I looked through the crowd for any of his followers or friends, but there was none to be seen. Then I saw her. The mother. Standing by a young, pock-faced boy. Why wasn't she shouting? Why didn't she scream out, 'Jesus!'? The mob would quickly follow her lead. The silence held. Then she leaned forward and whispered something to the boy. Suddenly he called out, splitting the silence asunder.

'Free Barabbas!' 'Free Barabbas!,' he shouted. Laughter started rippling through the crowd. People repeating the joke to their neighbours.

'Free Barabbas!' And the laughter increased, a flood of laughter, everybody taking up the joke till it echoed from the palace walls. 'Free Barabbas! Free Barabbas! Free Barabbas!'

I realised I was screaming, 'Free Jesus!' But nobody could hear through the hurricane of noise and laughter.

And the mother? The mother simply stood mute. Half a smile playing round her lips.

MARY. As I knelt crying at the foot of the cross I could feel her eyes. But I wouldn't even give her the benefit of a contemptuous look. She'd said such evil things to me after they'd taken Jesus away. Used gutter language, shamed me.

How dare she! How dare she suggest such a thing in public. As if I would have told the boy to shout Barabbas! All I said was 'I'm that man's mother.' And he said, 'Don't worry, old lady. I'll help set your son free.' And then he cried out 'Barabbas'.

A simple mistake, that's all. Or God's work.

MAGDALENE. He took too long to die. Soon they'd have to break his legs to finish him off. He didn't deserve to hurt that much. 'My God! My God! Why have you forsaken me?' he cried.

Finally I could bear it no more, and went and asked one of the soldiers to end it. I knew he was a good man at heart, I'd seen him pour the juice of the crushed poppy onto the vinegar-soaked sponge before touching Jesus' lips with it. But even good men have to be paid. The deal having been struck we went to the foot of the cross, and he stuck his spear in Jesus' side.

He looked down from the cross, saw me there and I think he knew that it was me who had brought this new pain to him. But his eyes were still full of love, forgiving, then he closed them; and it was over.

The soldier took me to a quiet place nearby. As I opened my legs, the tears finally came. He didn't notice. After all – as they say – I am simply a whore.

MARY. He's been dead for two days now. And tomorrow will rise. There are no doubts in my mind about that. God's will – will be done. I have no fears of the lies of the Magdalene . . . person. They have told me that the day the true story finally comes to be written – if she receives any mention at all – it will be simply in the passing. Her lies about me will not live beyond her. Which is only just. She is, after all, simply a whore.

MAGDALENE. She's waiting for him to be transferred to heaven in a beam of light now; so he can become some sort of a freakish god . . .

But he was just a man. A very special man; who . . . understood me. And that's how he shall always remain in my heart.

Some of them came to see me, the ones who've never liked me. Told me to stop talking about his mother. Stop telling 'lies' about her. Warned me to go away or face the consequences.

So I shall. Time to go home perhaps. To grow old – and wait to die. With joy in my heart at the thought of being together with him again.

They also told me, no one will hear my story after I am dead. Perhaps it's as well. Some truths are better left unspoken.

Long tail of wind and distant thunder.

DREAMS OF DUBLIN BAY

by Frank Dunne

To Kate

Frank Dunne is Irish. He has been an actor since the mid-fifties when he toured Ireland with Anew McMaster and played in Dublin seasons with the Edwards-MacLiammoir Company. In Britain he has worked extensively in the theatre and television. He began writing in the sixties and had early stories published in the Irish literary review *The Kilkenny Magazine*. He has had ten plays broadcast by RTE Radio in Ireland, all directed by William Styles. A number of his stories have been broadcast by BBC Radio 4 in their *Morning Story* slot. Two of his plays have been produced at the Lyric Theatre, Belfast: *The Rise and Fall of Barney Kerrigan* (1977) and *Old Days* (1981). In 1979 Collins published his children's novel *Wexford Road*. He now lives in Devon with his wife Eileen and his daughter Kate.

Dreams of Dublin Bay was first broadcast on BBC Radio 4 on 17 March 1987. The cast was as follows:

WILLIE/MAN	Sean Barrett
BABS	Pauline Delany
ANGELA	Alexandra Pigg
ROB	Paul Gregory
BEN	Neil Caple

Director: Peter Kavanagh
Running time, as broadcast: 27 minutes, 45 seconds

A full choir, backed by an organ, singing 'The Lord Is My Shepherd'. It fades as WILLIE *speaks.*

WILLIE (*his voice low, intimate*). My wife, Babs, moves to the sideboard. She picks up my photograph.

BABS. Poor Willie.

WILLIE. Gazes at my features.

BABS. God rest him.

WILLIE. A tear in her eye. (*We hear a little sob from* BABS.) A tear in the other eye.

BABS. A good husband. Always kind.

WILLIE. Not true. And well she knows it. Still now's not the time to say such things.

ANGELA. Sit down, Mum.

WILLIE. My daughter, Angela.

BEN. Yes, sit down, Mum. You'll only upset yourself.

WILLIE. My son, Ben.

ROB. That's right, sit down.

WILLIE. And Angela's husband, Rob. Big rugby-playing know-all. Successful in business, a tower of strength at lock forward.

BABS (*crying*). I couldn't have asked for a better husband.

WILLIE. You could. And often did.

BABS. I couldn't.

WILLIE. The first time I've ever seen her in black. It suits her. A pretty widow she'll make.

BABS. He – your father – your dear father – he was made for better things. He never really enjoyed being a teacher, you know.

WILLIE. I go along with that.

ANGELA. We all knew that, Mum.

WILLIE. How could you not help knowing it? Bringing my discontent home with me in the evenings. Filling the place with it.

BEN. Dad was a good teacher.

WILLIE. Was I?

BABS. He was. A very good teacher. Still. He never liked it.

ROB. It wasn't hard to see that.

WILLIE. Of course nothing's particularly hard for you to see, Rob. The world's a simple plot of land in your eyes. Whether at your accountant's desk or shoving and pushing your way round the scrum.

BABS. D'you know what his real ambition was?

WILLIE. No, Babs, no. Have a good cry or something, but keep all that to yourself.

BABS. His real ambition, your dad's real ambition was to be a writer.

WILLIE *groans.*

BEN. I never knew that.

ANGELA. And I didn't.

ROB. I certainly didn't.

BABS. Oh, yes, that's where his real ambition lay.

ANGELA. He never said anything about it.

BABS. Well, you know your father, Angela. He wasn't a man to talk about himself. But, yes, he wanted one time to be a writer.

WILLIE. If I was there among them I'd strangle her for saying that. Now, it doesn't seem to matter.

ROB. Why did he never do anything about it?

BABS. Oh, he did, Rob, he did. In his young days in Dublin.

ANGELA. Really?

BABS. He – he chucked his first teaching job and went to London.

BEN. He often talked about his London days.

WILLIE. The room off the Cromwell Road. Then the room in Belsize Park. Washing dishes in Joe Lyons. Humping scenery backstage at the Palladium. Supply teaching. A Kentish Town ten-year-old telling me to get stuffed in front of all the class.

BABS. He did various jobs. And wrote in the evenings.

WILLIE. Tried to, Babs, tried to. Didn't get very far. Well. Didn't get anywhere, if truth be told. But I made up for it. Consoled myself and got drunk in the West End. Met a girl called Kay.

BABS. He was very lonely. No friends, you see.

WILLIE. Except for Kay. But you wouldn't know about her, Babs.

ROB. And what did he write? Novels, plays? What?

WILLIE. That's right, Rob, get down to basics.

BABS. Oh, lots of things.

ANGELA. We never saw any of it.

ROB. Were they any good?

WILLIE. Excellent question, Rob.

BABS. Unfortunately he never kept any of his writings.

BEN. He travelled a lot. He told us.

BABS. All over Europe.

WILLIE. Hitchhiked. Slept rough in Paris. Ate cheaply in the boulevard St-Michel. Walked around the Louvre, the Jeu de Paume. Got a cheap ticket for Molière at the Comédie-Française. Thought I was – what? Educating myself. Bullshit like that.

ROB. So – what it comes down to is – he never really did anything about trying to be a writer?

WILLIE. Good man, Rob. Let no one off the hook.

BABS. Yes, he did, oh, yes, he did. He kept a diary of all his travels and went home to Dublin to work on it. Hoping, d'you see, to turn it into a travel book.

ANGELA. In Granny's house.

WILLIE. Our old home in Sandymount. Staunch Church of Ireland household. Bible texts on the walls, services and hymns on the BBC. A last pocket of loyalty to the King of England. A few streets away the strand and the sea looking to Howth. Dublin Bay. The sun across the water in the evening.

BEN. D'you remember, he showed us Granny's house when we went that time to Dublin.

BABS. Your granny was long dead by that time, Ben.

ROB. What I want to know is – what happened to the diary?

BABS. Poor Willie found he couldn't do anything with it. Not then.

WILLIE. The mass of materials was shapeless. It lay on my mother's kitchen table, a big wodge of paper, out of which any form refused to be extracted.

ANGELA. He came to England again after Granny died.

BABS. And got the school here in Liverpool. I was already nursing here. We met at a dance. I remember the night well.

WILLIE. In black, she moves weeping to the photograph again. Weeping, picks it up.

We hear a sob from BABS.

BABS. We started going out. One night he told me about the diary. He promised to bring it with him on our next date.

WILLIE. I did. I brought it.

BABS. I took it home with me. (*Crying.*) I remember sitting up reading it.

ANGELA. Come on, Mum, sit down. Don't distress yourself.

WILLIE. Angela persuades her to the armchair.

BABS. I – I told him how good I thought it was.

ROB. The diary?

BABS. Yes.

WILLIE. She did. She gave me renewed energy to try and make a book of it. To give her something back I asked her to marry me.

BABS. We were married here. Holy Trinity Church. (*Sobbing.*) A sunny June Saturday.

ANGELA. Oh, come on now, Mum.

WILLIE. All I remember of the day was the new shirt I was wearing. It was a half size too tight in the collar. Nearly choked me, I kept wanting to rip it off.

BABS. He worked so hard on his book after we were married. (*Sobbing.*) When I – When I think of him sitting in the evenings at the dining-room table.

WILLIE. The diary, the work on it in the evenings and the carrot of publication dangling ahead carried yours truly through the drudgery of school, through the birth of Angela.

ANGELA. You're only upsetting yourself, Mum, going on like this.

WILLIE. Through the birth of Ben.

BEN. That's right, Mum, it's no good going over the past.

WILLIE. With the sunshine of possible publication on my back things didn't seem too bad.

ROB. I suppose it was never published, the diary.

ANGELA. Oh, Rob, don't keep on at her. Can't you see she's upset remembering?

BABS. No, unfortunately – (*Slight sob.*) – it was never published. I made him send it out to publishers again and again.

WILLIE. She did. Give her her due. But back it came. The rejection slip a regular visitor through the letter box. A little more ragged, a little more battered each time.

ANGELA. Whatever happened to it?

BEN. I'd like to have read it.

WILLIE. And with the cares of looking after two children and the worry of making ends meet, Bab's interest in the diary began to ebb. And who could blame her?

BABS. In the end he gave up writing. I tried to encourage him to keep on.

WILLIE. One day I looked at the grubby typescript and the snappy letter back with it and I says to Babs, I says, 'That's the end, I'll not submit to any more publishers.' A year or two earlier she wouldn't have heard of such a thing. Now all she said was, 'Oh, really?' She was, d'you see, more concerned with Ben's potty problems at that particular moment.

BABS. I never really knew what happened to it.

WILLIE. Nor did I. It disappeared into some obscure corner or forgotten drawer.

Pause. A few quiet sobs from BABS.

ANGELA. Oh, Mum.

ROB (*whispering*). What's all this Angela's been telling me?

BEN (*whispering*). Telling you? What, Rob?

ROB (*whispering*). About his ashes going back to Dublin.

BEN (*whispering*). Mum's determined about it.

ROB (*whispering*). But why? And think of the damned expense.

BEN (*whispering*). It's to do with the will.

BABS. What's that?

ANGELA. What, Mum?

BEN. What, Mum?

BABS. What are they whispering about?

BEN. Nothing, Mum.

BABS. You were whispering.

BEN. Really, it was nothing.

ROB. Well, actually, I was just wondering –

ANGELA. Rob!

ROB. No, I must say it. Angela tells me you're thinking of taking his ashes back to Ireland.

BABS. To Dublin. Dublin Bay, to be exact.

ROB. But why?

BABS. It was his wish.

WILLIE. It was. And it seems so unimportant now.

ROB. But apart from the expense, which is bound to be considerable, think of the problems involved.

BABS. Problems? Problems, Rob?

ROB. Practical problems. And – and the upset. It will be such an upsetting experience for everyone.

BABS. You don't have to come, Rob.

ROB. I'm thinking of Angela. Frankly, this whole business has been such a shock for her. It being so sudden –

WILLIE. Sudden, that's right. A thud upstairs. Babs called out. No reply. She ran up. There I was.

ROB. Well, not to put too fine a point on it, I don't want her upset more than necessary.

ANGELA. Oh, be quiet, Rob, if Mum has to go, I'll go with her and that's all there is to it.

ROB. But why all that way, for God's sake? Why can't it – whatever it is – whatever you do –

BABS. What do you mean – whatever you do?

ROB. Well – whatever happens.

BABS. We scatter his ashes, that's what happens.

ROB. All right, why can't you scatter them here?

BABS. Because Willie wanted them scattered in Dublin. In Dublin Bay, to be accurate.

WILLIE. Yes, I did.

BABS. It was his one great wish in the last years of his life.

WILLIE. It was.

BABS. So strong did he feel about it that he specified it in his will.

WILLIE. True.

ROB. What? That his ashes were to be scattered in Dublin Bay?

BABS. Yes.

WILLIE. Yes.

ROB. But why? What's so special about Dublin Bay?

BABS. He always loved the view.

WILLIE. From Howth Head. Across to the Dublin Mountains and

the Wicklow Mountains. The Sugar Loaf. Clouds. Sea mists, rain blotting out the sky. And sunshine in summer, sparks of light on the water.

BEN. He took pictures of it when we went there as kids.

WILLIE. The sight of it a symbol of peace in my mind. Calm to the soul in times of distress.

BABS. I think it cheered him up thinking about it.

WILLIE. It did. Took me through – what? Oh, the long years. Long years in the one Liverpool school. Measured out my life there in dreams. All the comings and goings. Staff changes. While I stayed put. Same routine, same classroom. Part of the landscape. A bit of a joke to the cheekier kids. And the applications for headships, deputy headships, the half-hearted interviews. Knowing I wouldn't get them and, more to the point, not really wanting them. Sinking into the job. Dreaming no more.

ROB. Well, I think it's ridiculous.

WILLIE. Except that one dream.

BABS. It's not ridiculous, Rob. I won't have you saying that. It was what he wanted. He often told me so.

WILLIE. Dreams of Dublin Bay. Great balm to the tired soul, that thought. The Bible texts, the memory of childhood hymns, when resorted to were found wanting. But – rest in the green bay. With that ahead, at the finishing line, so to speak, life became tolerable.

BEN. Dad said once if he was buried in Liverpool he'd come back and haunt us.

WILLIE. Christ, yes, I forgot that.

ROB. Don't you think it was a trifle morbid? Being obsessed with – well, with where his ashes should rest.

BABS. D'you know, Rob, I felt like that at times. I told him so.

WILLIE. She did.

BABS. Morbid was the very word I used. Frankly, I didn't like to think of such things.

WILLIE. Gave her an eerie twinge, she said.

BABS. Gave me an eerie feeling. I mean, I said, who was to say I wouldn't go first?

WILLIE. First or last, I told her, my end must be the same.

ANGELA. That's why he told us, I expect. So that if he was the one left behind, Ben and I would know his wishes.

BABS. But now that – that it's happened, I don't think it's at all morbid. His great desire, that is, for his ashes to be scattered in Dublin Bay. In fact, and he'd laugh if he knew it, I believe now it's most important to carry out his wishes to the last detail.

WILLIE. I thought it was important too. And it was – in the sense that it served its purpose. It got me through – what? Life, I suppose. That old backyard bracketed by birth and death. But the joke is, Babs, it's not at all important now. Now, d'you see, that its purpose is ended. How can I tell you that? To save you all the trouble and the expense. And at the same time make cost-conscious Rob happy. And would you listen if I did tell you? Probably not. For it'd be impossible to demonstrate to you what I didn't know then but do now, that it – what you intend to scatter on the waters of Dublin Bay – has nothing to do with me now. Just a collection of particles of no concern to me. Isn't that funny? I'm sure you'd find it funny too, Babs, if I could get it across to you, if I – hey, wait, where the hell are you? Where have you all – ? Oh, my God, I've found them. There they all are on board an Aer Lingus aircraft drifting high up halfway across the Irish Sea.

BABS. I'm not happy, you know, about the – the – it being in the luggage compartment.

ANGELA. Where did you want us to put it, Mum? In my handbag?

BABS. Don't be frivolous, Angie. Especially at a time like this.

ROB (*whispering*). I've never been on a more absurd bloody expedition.

BEN (*whispering*). Well, Mum was determined and there was no talking her out of it.

ROB. I mean, I've taken two days off already. The day it happened and the funeral. And now there's today. And by rights I should be at a briefing in Birmingham this afternoon.

ANGELA. It's quite safe, Mum. Ben packed it securely in the cardboard box.

WILLIE. They leave the plane. Ben – look at him – carries a cardboard box tied with twine. They are getting into a car. Self-drive hire. Rob driving.

BABS. Watch out for the signs to Howth, Rob.

ANGELA. There! That says Howth.

BEN. It also says – what's that other name? (*Slowly:*) Balbriggan.

BABS. Take it.

WILLIE. After half an hour they stop, lost among fields.

ROB. What do I do now? Where do I go?

BABS. You should have turned right at that last turning.

ROB. There was no sign.

ANGELA. There was no sign, Mum.

ROB. I can't see the sea anywhere.

BEN. I think we're miles from the sea.

ANGELA. Ask this fellow.

ROB. Excuse me, sir.

MAN. Good-day.

ROB. Good-day.

MAN. Good-day, ma'am.

BABS. Good-day.

MAN. Good-day, miss.

ANGELA. Good-day.

MAN. A very nice, close day.

ANGELA. Very.

BEN. Could you tell us how we get to Howth, please?

MAN. Oh, God, sir, ye're miles off Howth.

ROB. You see!

MAN. Howth's that direction. Whereas ye're on the Drogheda road.
    Ye've no call to be on the Drogheda road if Howth's the
    destination ye're aiming for.

ROB. Well, what road should we be on?

MAN. Well, now, sir, ye'll have to turn round, go for about six miles
    down in that direction 'til ye come to a cross.

ANGELA. A cross?

BABS. Yes. A wayside crucifix. They have them all over Ireland.

MAN. No, ma'am. A crossroads.

BABS. Oh, I see.

MAN. Well, more of a junction, ma'am. Take the left fork, sir.

ROB. That will take us to Howth?

MAN. It will, sir. After you've turned right at Donaghty's pub and
    kept left when you get to McLaughlin's cross.

ROB. Oh, God!

BABS. Go on, Rob. We'll find it. Thank you.

MAN. Thank you, ma'am. And good-day.

BABS. Good-day.

MAN. Good-day, miss.

ANGELA. Good-day.

WILLIE. A few miles down the road they turn right, then left at McLaughlin's cross, on and on, but where is Howth?

ROB. I haven't a bloody clue where we are.

BABS. Language, Rob, please. Kindly remember why we're here. And – and the box on Ben's lap.

WILLIE. Driving on.

ANGELA. Look!

ROB. What?

ANGELA. The signpost.

WILLIE. Howth, six miles. They get out at Howth Harbour. Ben stumbles as he leaves the car.

BABS. Ben!

ANGELA. Ben!

BEN. Ooh, that was close! My rugby handling came in handy.

BABS. Ben, please! A little more respect.

ANGELA. What do we do now?

BABS. What do you think we do? We go out and – and – do what we have to do on the water.

BEN. What do you mean, go out, Mum?

BABS. Out to sea.

ROB. Out to sea. How? Swim?

BABS. No. I suppose we need a boat.

ROB. Where are we going to find a boat?

ANGELA. Yes, Mum, where are we going to find a boat? We should have arranged all that beforehand.

BABS. Well, we'll just have to do it from the shore then.

BEN. From here?

BABS. No, we'll go out on that cluster of rocks.

ROB. We'll break our necks.

BABS. Not if we're careful.

WILLIE. Stepping cautiously, with care, along the uneven rocks.

BABS (*screaming*). Oh!

WILLIE. Babs slips on seaweed. Is caught by Angela.

ANGELA. All right, Mum?

BEN. All right?

BABS (*a bit breathless*). Yes, yes, all right.

WILLIE. Reaching the end of the rocks. Waves lapping their feet.

ROB. The wind is blowing from the south.

ANGELA. What about it?

ROB. It's blowing in our faces.

ANGELA. I know it is. What about it?

ROB. You'll have to be careful how you – scatter the – how you do it.

ANGELA. Oh, yes!

ROB. Otherwise it'll all blow back on us.

ANGELA. You're right, Rob.

ROB (*whispering*). I don't relish the thought of brushing your dad out of my hair.

ANGELA (*whispering*). Shut up!

BABS. We're all right here. Untie the box, Ben.

BEN. I can't. If I untie it with one hand it'll unbalance off the other.

ANGELA. You hold it, Ben. I'll untie it.

WILLIE. Angela does that.

ANGELA. There! Now, Rob, you take out the – you know.

ROB. Me?

ANGELA. Yes.

WILLIE. Rob does as instructed.

ROB. What do I do with it?

BABS. Open it, of course. Then hand it to me.

WILLIE. Rob pulls at the lid.

ROB (*straining*). It won't – it won't open.

ANGELA. You're sure you've got the right end?

ROB (*tetchily*). Of course I've got the right end.

ANGELA. Let me try.

WILLIE. And Angela tries.

ANGELA (*straining*). No. No good. No.

BABS. You try, Ben.

BEN (*straining*). No, I can't undo it.

BABS (*upset*). What shall we do?

ROB. Couldn't you throw it in without opening it?

BABS. You know, Rob, you're very irritating at times.

ROB. Why?

BABS. My husband asked specifically for his ashes to be scattered on the waters.

WILLIE. So I did.

ROB. Well, they will be scattered. It's just that the casket won't be open.

BABS. If the casket won't be open his ashes can't be scattered. Can they? Use your common sense.

ANGELA. We can't stand here all day.

BEN. I'm frozen.

ROB. The water is rising.

ANGELA. And we have a plane to catch back to Manchester tonight.

BABS. Try again, Ben.

WILLIE. Ben tries.

BEN. No good, Mum. It's jammed. Stuck.

BABS. What are we going to do?

ANGELA. Maybe Rob's right, Mum. Maybe you should throw it in as it is.

BABS. But we won't be carrying out your father's wishes.

ANGELA. We've tried hard enough to carry out his wishes. Flying over here, getting lost in the middle of nowhere, nearly killing ourselves and catching pneumonia out on these rocks.

BABS. And so you should. He was a good father to you.

ANGELA. I know he was.

WILLIE. Do you? You questioned it once or twice in your teens, I remember.

ANGELA. But we've done our best, Mum.

BEN. It's true what she says, Mum. If I were you I'd throw it in as it is and have done with it.

BABS. Have done with it! That's a nice way to speak. It seems to me you're all only too eager to have done with your father.

ROB. Well, I'm standing here no longer. The water's lapping round my socks.

BABS. Oh, give it here to me.

WILLIE. Babs takes it. Stumbles.

ANGELA (*screaming*). Hold on to her, Ben.

BEN. O.K., Mum, I've got you.

ANGELA. All right, Mum. Now.

BABS (*sobbing*). Goodbye, dear Willie.

WILLIE. Babs throws.

ROB. Oh, God, no, look where it's landed.

ANGELA. On that bit of rock in the water.

BEN. We'll never reach it.

ROB. You didn't throw hard enough.

ANGELA. Never mind, the tide will carry it out.

BABS. No, no, we have to put it in the sea.

ANGELA. It *will* be in the sea, Mum, in about ten minutes.

ROB. We'll all be in the bloody sea if we don't move.

BABS. We have to do it, we have to.

ANGELA. Rob, do you see that stick? See if you can reach it with that.

ROB. It's covered with green, seaweedy slime.

ANGELA. It won't kill you! You get it, Ben. I'll hold on to Mum.

WILLIE. Ben balances his way to the stick, takes it up, brings
    it back.

ANGELA. Try to push it into the water.

BABS. Do be careful, oh, do be careful.

BEN. Don't worry, Mum. I won't fall in.

BABS. It's not you I'm worried about. It's – it's him.

BEN. Hold on to me someone.

ROB. Here, I will.

WILLIE. Ben lunges with the stick. Misses. (ANGELA *screams.*) Slips
    down rocks.

ANGELA. Hold on, hold on to him, Rob.

ROB. I am. I'm holding on.

BEN. I was nearly in that time.

ANGELA. You try, Rob.

WILLIE. Ben gives the stick to Rob. Rob takes careful aim. Strikes.

ANGELA. You've moved it.

WILLIE. Rob too is moved. He overbalances and goes up to his
    knees in water.

ROB. Blast!

ANGELA. Language, Rob, language!

BEN. Look. It's bobbing gently.

BABS. Goodbye, dear, goodbye.

ROB. Help me up someone.

ANGELA. It's just there. Hardly moving.

BEN. Bobbing.

ANGELA. Gently.

ROB. For Christ's sake, could someone give me a hand?

BABS. It's as if – as if he doesn't want to leave us.

The gentle sound of the sea.

WILLIE. Drifting. Ebbing, flowing in the Dublin Bay currents. The winter spent wandering back and forth between Howth and Dalkey. Many were the hard knocks from passing craft. Once, propelled for over a mile by the Mail Boat out of Dun Laoghaire, a vessel upon which I had often travelled in years gone by. Gradually floating away from land and coming out into the open sea. Often a seagull perched there, but finding the perch less steady than expected would fly off again. Fish occasionally had a nibble and for months an old baked-bean can attached itself to a corner and only came loose in the violence of a November storm.

The loud crash of waves.

Currents, winds, wild waves driving across the Irish Sea. Lingering along the North Wales coast, getting entangled with sewage from Llandudno and pollution from factories in Flintshire. Smeared by oil from a tanker off Prestatyn, knocked about by yachtsmen from Colwyn Bay.

A ship's horn.

Easing along grimy water towards Birkenhead. Passing Crosby and Bootle, floating up the Mersey.

Ship's horns, engine noises, pneumatic drills, etc.

Construction work afoot in the busy dockland, concrete being laid, extending the quay for the Liverpool–Dublin ferry. Floating on. Mingling with old bits of concrete, loosened by pneumatic drills and splashing into the basin among cardboard packets, tin cans, broken boots, tyres, bits of wood, oil slicks. Moving nearer the quay. A large mechanically controlled vat of wet concrete is about to be emptied into a drilled out hole beside the water. A squat tug chugs by. The strong wash from it thrashes the water about. Waves clash. Up out of the water. High. And flung into the hole, alongside a soggy Kleenex box, a piece of broken

orange crate and an old programme of an Everton game at
Highbury. The vat empties its load of wet concrete into the hole.
Ten minutes later another load of wet concrete comes down.
A few more loads and the hole is filled in. The concrete is
smoothed on top and at the side and a large section of the quay
has acquired a new face. And under the new face is – (WILLIE's
laughter begins.) Locked into Liverpool forever.

WILLIE's *laughter. It fades slowly. Pause.*

ANGELA. Every year on that day Mum travels to Dublin. She insists
on it.

BABS. I insist on it.

ANGELA. Ben and myself take turns going over with her.

BEN. We take turns.

BABS. That one day. Every year.

BEN. We take the boat from that new dock in Liverpool.

ANGELA. That nice new dock.

BEN. We arrive in Dublin.

ANGELA. Hire a car to Howth.

The sound of the sea.

BEN. And stand on those rocks jutting into the water.

ANGELA. We look out across Dublin Bay.

BEN. And remember Dad.

ANGELA. We remember our father.

BABS. Standing there – it's strange – he seems, Willie seems so
close to us again.

WILLIE's *laughter begins and builds. After a while 'The Lord Is
My Shepherd' fades up.*

NOBBY'S DAY

by Anna Fox

For the children of Bank End School

Nobby's Day is Anna Fox's second radio play, her first being *Relics*, transmitted a year earlier. Born in India, she travelled extensively with her family before coming home to England and going to school, which she left at sixteen to train as an actress at RADA. Her first job was touring with Stephen Joseph's Theatre in the Round playing Panope in *Phèdre* with Margaret Rawlings; later joining the resident company – then in its infancy – in Scarborough. She played three years in repertory at Southport, Manchester and Salisbury where she married and started a family. A London run of *The Case in Question* followed at the Haymarket Theatre, and afterwards a short season with the Royal Shakespeare Company. Appearances on television include Odette in *Roads to Freedom*, Pamela in *The Brothers*, and Clemmie in *Jennie*. She lives in Hampstead with her husband, actor Christopher Benjamin, with whom she has three children.

Nobby's Day was first broadcast on BBC Radio 4 on 9 June 1987. The cast was as follows:

NOBBY	Richard Perry
BRIAN	Struan Rodger
MARY	Barbara Marten
GRANDAD	George Malpas
GRAN	Frances Cox
MR HORNE	Steve Hodson
MR POLLIT	John Graham Davies
MR GODBER/HOUSEHOLDER	Russ Elias
MISS TROTTMAN/1ST WOMAN	Pauline Jefferson
MRS PECK/2ND WOMAN	Rita May
JASON	Neil Scanlan
JONATHAN	Kerry Dougherty
RACHEL	Zoe Gill
1ST GIRL	Natalie Orrell
2ND GIRL	Sarah Johnson

Director: Jane Morgan
Running time, as broadcast: 50 minutes, 31 seconds

Distant sounds of a typically English sea-side scene: children's laughter,
seagulls, the tide's ebb and flow. One imagines an endless stretch of sand and sea.
Gradually the swish of a windsurfer carving through the water comes closer and
then very close. Abruptly it cuts off and gives precedence to the ticking of an
ancient bedside alarm clock in a silent room. A door opening, the rattle of a tea
cup and a shuffle of boots on a wooden floor indicate that NOBBY *is carrying a*
cup of tea with great care. We feel physically very close to NOBBY *during the*
initial action – his breathing, sniffing, clothes rustling, a click of annoyance as
the tea slops into the saucer and, finally, his hushed voice as he bends close to
GRAN's *sleeping face. The sea-side sounds are reference to* GRAN's *dream she*
is at this moment enjoying.

NOBBY. Gran. Wake up, Gran. Gran. Shall I draw curtains?

GRAN (*murmurs into consciousness*). Norman, where are you? That
you, Norman?

   NOBBY *crosses the floor to draw back the curtains.*

NOBBY. No, it's Nobby.

GRAN. Where are you? What have they done to me?

NOBBY. It's morning time. I brought a cuppa tea.

GRAN. Where's me teeth? Fetch me teeth.

NOBBY. They're in beaker.

GRAN. How can I sup tea wi'out me teeth?

   NOBBY *is reluctant to handle her dentures.*

NOBBY. Shall I give you t'beaker then?

GRAN. Aye.

   GRAN *sloshes around for her teeth.*

NOBBY (*sternly*). Won't you sit up a bit, Gran?

GRAN. Where are they?

NOBBY. You're holding them.

GRAN finds her teeth and inserts them.

GRAN. Now. Where's me glasses?

NOBBY. Here's your glasses.

GRAN. Oh aye, that's it.

She dons her specs.

Now then. I'm ready.

Rattling the cup on the saucer.

Not up there, I can't hold it up there. Bring it down. That's it.
Now then. This is better.

As GRAN enjoys a sip of tea, NOBBY heads discreetly for the door.

Nobby. Where are you going?

NOBBY. T'have me breakfast.

GRAN. Come here.

NOBBY. I gorra go t'school, Gran.

GRAN. Come here.

NOBBY approaches the bed.

Wait 'til I've supped me tea.

NOBBY. I'll be late for school.

GRAN. No you won't.

NOBBY. Aye, I will.

GRAN. I need the pan.

NOBBY. Me mum does it.

GRAN. I'm not comfortable. Straighten quilt.

NOBBY brushes the quilt with the flat of his hand.

I had such a funny dream, Nobby. I were on water. Oceans of it
all stretching, stretching. And I were moving fast. I were
skimming, skimming across all this water. And th'were a pier – all
sticking out and covered in sunshine. I wanted to get on it, but I
couldn'a. It came up close, but I just passed it by.

NOBBY crosses purposefully to the door and opens it.

Where have you gone? Nobby?

NOBBY (*mumbles*). I'm g'in 'ave me breakfast.

*The door closes and NOBBY's boots clatter down the stairs. Another door
bursts open to the muted sounds of breakfast television.*

Y'got me conkers ready, Grandad?

GRANDAD (*flustered*). Aye, aye, aye, aye. Up there on the jolly
'orner. Watch me dibbles. I said watch me . . .

NOBBY *snatches a handful of conkers and makes a dive back to the door.*

(*Calling:*) I'll be needing more twine if you're wanting more done.

A light object falls on to the hearth. The door bangs.

Oh . . . look at that.

The kitchen door opens where MARY *is frying bread.*

MARY (*exasperated almost beyond endurance*). Where have you been?
Where have you been?

NOBBY. Nowhere.

MARY. Sit down. Did Gran get her tea?

NOBBY. Aye.

MARY. Well?

NOBBY. What?

MARY. What kept you?

NOBBY. Nowt.

MARY. They're not going to take much more, you know.

NOBBY. What?

MARY. At school. Punctuality I'm talking about, punctuality. It's all
very well for you but I'm the one who gets told off, you know.
What were you doing upstairs, I only asked you to take her a cup
of tea. Oh, go on, eat your bacon.

NOBBY. She wanted her teeth.

MARY. Well she knows where they are, she knows I put them in a
beaker by her bed. Don't bolt it like that, Nobby. I've told her,
when she wakes up she only has to stretch out her hand and
there's her teeth all ready waiting for her. Nobby, don't you dare
feed that dog. Get out. Go on. Out.

MARY *shoos the dog out.*

Bacon costs good money.

She slams the door.

NOBBY. It were only a scrap.

MARY (*relenting*). Come on, eat your bread and butter. I suppose she
asked you for the bed pan. Well. Did she?

NOBBY. Aye.

MARY. All right love. (*She kisses him.*) I'll get up to your Gran now. Finish your bread and butter and get off quick. There's your packed lunch. Football boots are in the porch.

She is on her way out.

And put your blazer on.

The front door slams and NOBBY *runs down the path and onto the pavement where he collides with his father,* BRIAN.

BRIAN. Watch it, watch it. Eh. (*He tries to grab at him.*) Bloody hell, what time do you call this?

NOBBY. Gerroff, Dad, I'm going t'school.

BRIAN. Aye, but what bloody time do you call it? (*Roaring after him.*) Nobby. Nobby, you're dropping summat out your satchel. (*To himself:*) Oh my God, it's bloody sandwiches. (*Calling.*) Put them in your pocket, lad, in your pocket. (*Under his breath:*) Oh God help us. (*Calling:*) Gi' 'em a brush before you . . . (*To himself:*) Nay, what's the point? (*Yelling:*) You're all right now, then?

NOBBY. Aye.

BRIAN. Run, lad, you're late.

The front door closes and BRIAN *is inside now. He takes off his coat and hangs it up.*

MARY (*from upstairs*). Is that you, Brian?

BRIAN. What bloody time is that to leave for school?

MARY. It's not my fault, he dithers.

The lavatory chain is pulled some way off. A pained squeal from the dog.

BRIAN. Bloody dog. Get out, go on. Come here, go on. (*Opening the front door.*) Outside. (*He slams it.*)

MARY (*from the top of the stairs, highly exasperated*). Oh Brian, you've not let Bosun out.

BRIAN. That dog deliberately tripped me up. I've not come home to get my bloody neck broken.

MARY. He'll only follow Nobby.

BRIAN. How many times has that boy been late this week?

MARY (*from the top of the stairs*). He's a good lad.

BRIAN. He's a bloody mental case. He's left half his packed lunch in road.

MARY. He what?

BRIAN. His packed lunch. He's shedding sandwiches all down road.

MARY. Why?

BRIAN. How should I know? They were all coming out his satchel.

MARY. I didn't put them in his satchel.

BRIAN (*viciously*). I don't suppose you did. If his mother had put them in, they wouldn't be coming out, would they?

MARY (*nearer*). What's up?

BRIAN. Pit's closing.

MARY. No.

BRIAN. That's what they want.

BRIAN *opens a door.*

How's yoursen, Grandad?

GRANDAD. Not too bad, not too bad.

BRIAN. Sharp frost outside.

GRANDAD. Don't you think I don't know, it's degrees colder.

BRIAN. Keep wrapped up.

GRANDAD (*hesitantly*). I could do wi' a drop more coal in here, you know.

BRIAN. Aye, well I'm g'in 'ave me breakfast now. I'll see t' it later.

GRANDAD. Aye, aye, tha's done a hard night's work, lad.

BRIAN (*briskly*). Back later.

The door closes sharply.

GRANDAD. Tha' deserves a good breakfast.

NOBBY'*s footsteps running along the pavement cross over in to the wood where leaves and twigs crackle softly underfoot. The satchel thumps rhythmically on his back and his breath comes in pants. Bosun's bark is heard.* NOBBY *stops and gasps in desperation.*

NOBBY (*calling*). Bosun. Go home, Bosun.

Bosun reaches NOBBY *and is presumably greeting him.*

Naughty boy, Bosun, naughty boy. Stop it.

Tussling sounds and Bosun doggy panting.

Get down.

A commotion among the leaves and Bosun barks sharply, waiting for a stick to be thrown.

I can't throw a stick now, I can't. (*Imitating his father:*) Go home. Go on. (*A short bark.*) All right then, I'll throw you a stick. Now, when I throw this stick, you can go home. Do you promise?

NOBBY *throws a stick for all he's worth.*

(*Shouting:*) Catch it.

And runs on rapidly.

(*Breathlessly talking to himself:*) Quick. Run.

He trips and falls. A reflective pause. NOBBY *sits up in a pile of dry leaves.*

(*Tearfully:*) I've fallen over now.

Bosun gallops up and tramples all over him, licking his face.

Gerroff, stop licking me. Bad dog.

NOBBY *scrambles up.*

(*Enticingly:*) Eh, Bosun. I've got some lovely sandwiches here, Bosun. Crab paste and all. (*Rustling the paper.*) You've gorra stay on guard . . . or there'll be no packed lunch for yer. Sit. (*Alarmed:*) SIT.

Bosun jumps up and makes a snatch at the sandwiches amid much paper crackling and tussling.

(*Shouting:*) No. No. Gerroff.

Fading.

Yer can't take them all.

Fade out.

Sounds of the usual preliminary chaos before the first lesson of the morning. A crowded class of potentially willing seven-year-olds.

MR HORNE. Settle down, settle down. Rita, fetch me that big red book behind you. No, behind you. Rachel, can you show her? That's it. Thank you, Rachel. No, Jason, I did not say you could sit with Jonathan again. No, you are not sitting with Jonathan 'til you have proved you can stay quiet for five minutes. Go on, back to your place. Now then. Are we all here at last? Good. Right. Now, we are going to find out about trees today. Can anyone tell me what those trees are outside the window? Who is that looking in? Bye! That were quick, he's vanished. Who were that boy looking in through the window?

A chorus of 'Nobby Taylor'.

Nobby Taylor. What's he doing coming to school at this time?

There is a commotion at the door.

All right, Nobby, come on in. Come on in, lad. Now what kept you this time? You're all right, are you? Oh now then, come on, lad, it's not that serious.

NOBBY *is gulping copiously.*

Oh dear, oh dear. Look, it's not the end of the world, lad. There we are, then. Rachel, fetch a drink of water. Quick. All right, Nobby, all right. Come on, get a grip on yourself, you've not committed a crime. Hurry up with that water, please Rachel. What is it, Nobby? Try and tell me what it is, lad, come on, we can't have this can we? Spill it out.

NOBBY *tries to speak, but can't manage it.*

Go and ask Miss Bolt for a box of tissues, Jason. Do not run. Walk slowly. Oh, here's Rachel with a drink of water. Thank you Rachel, that was very kind of you. Here we are, Nobby, take a good drink, lad.

NOBBY *drinks noisily.*

That's better.

A deep inhalation of breath from NOBBY.

Oh my word, that's better. That's done the trick, hasn't it? Don't crowd round now, everybody, give him a chance. Easy, Jason, let him breathe. Three or four tissues will be quite sufficient. Big blow, Nobby. Yes, Rachel, I believe he has finished his water, go on, you can take the cup. Right, Nobby, better now?

A short silence while NOBBY *nods assent.*

Can you tell me what was wrong?

NOBBY (*practically inaudible*). Can't go to games.

MR HORNE. What, after break? Football?

NOBBY. Aye.

MR HORNE. You've not hurt yourself, have you?

NOBBY. No.

MR HORNE. Why can't you go to games then?

NOBBY. Got no boots.

Sounds of MARY *washing up at the sink. She is shaken by* BRIAN'*s news of the closure. An intense scene, each searching for clues as to how the other feels, yet neither able to contain their anger.*

BRIAN. Will you look at what this dog's been rolling in. It's caked in it. It's that lad should be doing this. It's Nobby's job, is this. Who told you to go dead, dog? You're soft aren't you? Stand up, come on, up. I can't get at you down there.

MARY *comes nearer to the table where* BRIAN *is sitting.*

MARY. Finished your tea?

BRIAN. No, no. Leave it.

MARY. Five hundred men.

BRIAN. It's not final.

MARY. They closed Fryston. And Kinfield.

BRIAN. Aye, well that's Fryston and Kinfield.

MARY. Tell me why Darthorpe should be different?

BRIAN. There's ways we can keep going, we can juggle around.

MARY. Juggle around. What are you then, clowns in circus?

BRIAN. You know nowt about it, so you can keep your bloody
nose out.

MARY. Tell me then, I want to know. I want to know.

BRIAN. You know nowt about it.

MARY. What can be done then, Brian?

BRIAN. For a start we can take coal underground t'washery at
Warmsley, they can blend it wi' other coal and get output up that
way, there's ways and means. (*In anguish:*) They can't write us off
yet, we're still productive. (*Suddenly defeated:*) Look what you've
done now. Frightened dog.

MARY. Couldn't you talk to them? Won't they listen to you?

BRIAN. Listen! (*Kindly:*) No, love. Clueless bloody question, that is.
There's not one in management's got the nous to take the long
view. Short-term measures, time after time. And it's daft. 'Cos
we'll always need coal.

A primary-school playground rumpus: skipping/football. This is break.

NOBBY. Over here, Jason, over here.

A kick. NOBBY is reluctant to part with the ball.

JASON. Back to me, back to me. Give over, Nobby.

JONATHAN. Give over, Nobby.

RACHEL. You're not allowed to play football in the playground.

JONATHAN. Shut thee gob!

RACHEL. Mi . . . er! (*She is pulling a face.*)

JASON. Kick it.

A kick. A pause. A short squeal of brakes.

JONATHAN (*awed*). It's gone over wall.

JASON. Go and gerrit.

JONATHAN. You go an gerrit.

JASON. I'm not going. You go Nobby.

NOBBY (*knowing he'll have to*). I can't.

JASON. Go on.

NOBBY (*apprehensively*). I can't.

JASON. Go on, you kicked it.

NOBBY. You gorra wait for me, then.

> NOBBY *struggles to open the gates, big iron ones. They groan on their hinges.*

RACHEL (*bursting with self-righteousness*). I told you.

JONATHAN. Shurrup, Rachel.

RACHEL. Mr Pollit'll find out.

JASON.
JONATHAN. } SHURRUP.

> *Sounds of* NOBBY's *footsteps running in the street.*

MR GODBER. Stop that boy. (*Shouting.*)

1ST WOMAN (*close*). Poor old dog.

2ND WOMAN (*close*). Does he know what he's done, that lad? Is that dog dead?

1ST WOMAN. He damned near caused a accident, never mind dog.

MR GODBER (*shouting*). You won't get far.

> *Back to muted playground noises.*

RACHEL. You'll get housemarks.

JASON. You dare tell Mr Pollit.

RACHEL. I'm not going to tell him, he'll just find out, that's all.

JASON. You dare and I'll tell him you swung on climbing frame.

RACHEL. I didn't.

JASON. You did, I saw you.

RACHEL. It were Rosemary, yah.

> *The gate groans again as* NOBBY *returns, panting for breath.*

JONATHAN. Nobby's back.

NOBBY. There's a dog in road. It's been run over and all.

> *The bell rings signalling the end of break.*

JASON. Is it dead?

NOBBY. It's not moving.

JONATHAN. Is there blood coming out?

NOBBY. Aye, I think so.

JASON. It's dead, then.

JONATHAN. Gi' us the ball quick.

JASON (*already moving away*). Don't purrit in my locker.

A cursory knock on the door as BRIAN *walks into* GRAN's *bedroom.*

BRIAN. Hello, Mother.

GRAN. Brian?

BRIAN. Aye it's me.

> *He sits on the bed which squeaks a little.*

> Oh. (*He is shocked.*) Put your hands under sheets, they're blocks of ice. There now. How are you doing?

GRAN. I were all right this morning.

BRIAN. Oh aye.

GRAN. I had a dream.

BRIAN. A dream?

GRAN. I can't swim, you know, Brian.

BRIAN. No.

GRAN. It were like flying. Swerving round. (*She is living it.*) Eee, it were grand.

BRIAN. Having a good time, were you?

GRAN. And the sun were warm on me shoulders. Summertime. It were summertime.

BRIAN. Summertime, eh.

GRAN. And the sea were all silver.

BRIAN. That were a good dream.

GRAN. Aye.

BRIAN. You're all right, are you, Gran? In yoursen?

GRAN. Eh?

BRIAN. Comfortable, are you comfortable?

GRAN. I can't complain.

BRIAN. You look sharp and get well, then. Grandad's missing you.

GRAN. I wanted to get on pier. But it just passed me by.

BRIAN. Aye well. Right, bed for me now, Mother. Couple hours shuteye. Keep wrapped up, I'll look in again tonight.

Sounds of NOBBY's *class playing football in the field.*

MR HORNE. Come forward, Ian, forward. Right down, right down. Good. Now Jonathan, pass to Ian.

The ball is kicked.

That's it, that's it. Try for a goal.

Another kick. JASON, *playing goalie, hurls himself on top of the ball with excessive zeal. Lusty shouts of triumph.*

Well stopped, Jason. Get off him, get off him, we are not playing rugby. Get back, come on, get back. Come along Jason, that ball is not your personal property. Get rid of it, big kick.

A kick.

You'll not make Wembley tying up your bootlaces, Nobby.

Sounds of running.

Stay with it, Jonathan, keep your eye on it. Wake up, Nobby. Now, pass to Nobby. Now, now.

A kick.

Oh lord, flat on his face.

The whistle blows.

Hold it. Hang on, let's sort this out. (*Approaching:*) Now then, Nobby. What are we wearing, seven league boots?

NOBBY. No, Mark Lithgoe's.

MR HORNE. Mark Lithgoe, he's in class eight.

NOBBY. He said I could borrer them.

MR HORNE. Aye, but he's a hefty lad, is Mark Lithgoe. You can't hope to play football in them, Nobby.

NOBBY. I can.

MR HORNE. Look. Change places wi' Jason in goal. (*Calling:*) Jason, come and change wi' Nobby, I want him in goal. (*Surprised, to himself:*) Mr Pollit, what's he doing out here?

MR POLLIT (*from far away*). Mr Horne.

MR HORNE (*calling*). Be right with you Mr Pollit. (*To his boys:*) All right, lads, carry on. I'm going to have a word with Mr Pollit. Here we are, Jason, catch. (*He throws the ball.*) Take a corner. Nobby, you're goalie now, get moving.

MR HORNE *squelches off down the field while the lads resume their game.*

MR POLLIT (*far away*). Sorry to interrupt, Stanley, I wanted a word . . .

JASON. Eh. What's Mr Pollit doing up here?

JONATHAN. I don't know.

NOBBY (*shouting*). Take a corner, Jason.

JONATHAN. Come on Jason.

The ball is kicked. There is a good deal of scuffling and sloshing about.

JASON. Watch out, Nobby.

A kick, followed by jubilant shouts of 'goal'.

Sounds of subdued babbling from the assembly hall back at St Michael's. The entire school has gathered together and waits expectantly. There is a hush as MR POLLIT *mounts the rostrum.*

MR POLLIT. Now then girls and boys, I expect you are wondering what all this is about. Well, I've had some very disturbing news which concerns us all here at St Michael's. At approximately eleven o'clock this morning, outside in the street, a dog was struck by a football coming from the direction of the school premises. A boy was seen to leave the school in a furtive manner to collect the ball.

During the following sentence which is back projected, we are very close in on the exchange between the children.

I do not need to remind you that not only are ball games of any variety forbidden during break, but that the street outside the school is out of bounds during school hours.

RACHEL. I told you Mr Pollit would find out.

JASON. Shurrup, Rachel, I'll get you.

RACHEL. I didn't tell him.

JASON *punches* RACHEL.

RACHEL (*tearful but muted*). Ow. Gerroff, Jason.

MR POLLIT. Now, that boy knows perfectly well he has broken the rules, and consequently he knows what he must do. Let him not hesitate. He who hesitates is lost. I am going up to my study now where I shall wait for him. And I know that I shall not have to wait for very long. That is all.

MR POLLIT *walks off the rostrum and, after a moment, the babble returns.*

Silence. There is a prolonged but very soft knocking on the door of MR POLLIT'*s study.*

MR POLLIT. Come in.

The door opens clumsily and there is a curious adhesive sound when Mark Lithgoe's studs meet the parquet floor.

Nobby Taylor. Close the door.

The door closes.

Have you something you wish to tell me? (*Silence.*) Let me put it this way. Were you playing football during break this morning in the playground?

NOBBY. Aye.

MR POLLIT (*quickly*). Who with?

Silence.

All right, all right, we'll ignore that for the time being. Going out for that ball. Was it you, Nobby?

NOBBY (*hardly audible*). Aye. But . . (*Deep breathing.*)

MR POLLIT. But what, lad?

NOBBY. I didn't know . . . (*More breathing.*)

MR POLLIT (*very patiently*). Didn't know what?

NOBBY. . . . 'owt about dog.

MR POLLIT (*earnestly*). That is why we don't play football in the playground. That ball could have done untold damage. Now it so happens that it struck a dog. And most unfortunately, the dog belongs to Councillor Godber, governor of the board of this school.

NOBBY. Is he dead?

MR POLLIT. Who?

NOBBY. The dog.

MR POLLIT. No. The dog's all right.

NOBBY. I thought he were dead.

MR POLLIT. He's poorly, mind. A nasty lump on his head.

NOBBY (*bursting with relief*). Can I go now, Mr Pollit?

MR POLLIT. Go? Certainly not.

NOBBY. But he's not dead.

MR POLLIT. That doesn't make everything all right. You stay put, I've not finished with you by a long chalk. Now. (*Irritable:*) Nobby, I'm finding it very difficult keeping my eyes off your footwear. May I inquire why it is necessary to be walking about in football boots that patently belong to someone considerably larger than yourself?

RACHEL *and her crew are wending their way up the road munching crisps in an entirely desultory way.*

1ST GIRL. Is yours cheese and onion, Rachel?

RACHEL. Salt and vinegar.

2ND GIRL. I wanted salt and vinegar, he's given me smoky bacon.

RACHEL. He's done that before.

2ND GIRL. Swop yer salt and vinegar for smoky bacon?

1ST GIRL. I've got prawn cocktail.

RACHEL. I don't like prawn cocktail, it's fishy.

1ST GIRL. Scampi and lemon's fishy.

OTHERS. EEE – YER – AIR (*Tongues extended.*)

RACHEL (*brazen glee*). Eh. Halloween tonight.

> *Sounds of ghostly hoo-hooing followed by laughter. The theme is taken up and explored – possibly singing. Somebody pops their crisp bag, somebody else squeals loudly.*

2ND GIRL. Eh, look at them lads on that skip. They're not allowed on there.

RACHEL (*calling*). Are you trick and treating tonight, Jonathan?

JONATHAN. No.

RACHEL (*nearer*). Are you trick and treating, Nobby? We're coming up round your way tonight.

NOBBY. Don't know.

RACHEL. Ask your mum, then.

JASON (*calling from a little way off*). Come on.

RACHEL. Nobby. Do you like me?

> NOBBY *jumps into a pile of sand.*

1ST GIRL. You're not allowed to jump in that sand, Nobby.

RACHEL (*close*). Do you like me, Nobby?

NOBBY (*close*). Don't know.

> *The following exchange takes place with* NOBBY *moving about at various distances from the mike while* RACHEL *stays put.* NOBBY *is actually walking up a plank onto the skip where he leaps off and down onto a pile of sand.*

RACHEL. Do you like Janice?

NOBBY. No.

RACHEL. You do, you like Janice.

NOBBY. No I don't, she's daft is Janice.

RACHEL. Do you like me, then?

NOBBY. I quite like yer.

RACHEL. As much as Janice?

NOBBY (*pestered*). I don't like Janice.

RACHEL. She likes you.

> *There is a thump as* RACHEL *is hit with a dollop of sand.*

> Gerroff, Jason. You're not allowed to play with that sand.

JASON. Eh, look out, someone's coming.

> *A tremendous scrambling and scuffling and running of feet up the road.*

HOUSEHOLDER (*barely distinguishable at first*). Gerroff, bloody animals. I know where you come from, don't think I don't. If I catch you round here once more, I'll thrash living daylights out yer.

> *The running of feet is a long way off and gradually fades into nothing.*

> MARY *is washing up in the kitchen and humming to the strains of 'Down Town'. A door opens.*

MARY (*knows it is* NOBBY, *without turning round*). Hello, love, did you wipe your feet?

> *She turns, aghast.*

> No Nobby, no. Stay where you are, stay right there. Look at you. You're bright yellow. Is that builders' sand? Don't you know that it stains?

> *She dives at him and brushes his blazer.* NOBBY *almost falls over.*

NOBBY. Give over.

MARY. And you had a clean pully on this morning. (*She sighs.*) Oh Nobby. Sometimes I just want to give up. You forgot to take your football boots, didn't you? I told you, I said they were in the porch, I said your packed lunch is on the table and your boots are in the porch. Didn't I? Didn't I?

NOBBY *can't take much more.*

> What did you do without them?

NOBBY. Borrowed Mark Lithgoe's.

MARY. Mark Lithgoe's? You wore Mark Lithgoe's football boots?

NOBBY. They were all right.

MARY. The mind boggles. (*Disguising her amusement:*) Never mind love, eh, come on. Let's get your blazer off and I'll give it a brush over sink.

NOBBY. What's for tea?

MARY. Kippers. Take your satchel out of butter.

She swoops on the satchel and plucks it off the table.

Look, sit still a minute. Just . . . sit down and keep still a minute. Arms out. That's the way. And the other one. My God, just look at this blazer.

Brushing the blazer.

Listen love, you're going to have to put this on again. I want you to run up t' Trotty's for some sugar. Two pound of sugar and a packet of tea.

NOBBY. I'm hungry.

MARY. You can tuck straight in when you come back.

NOBBY. I want some bread.

MARY. Come on, put your arm through, it won't take a minute.

NOBBY. Just one piece.

MARY. Now the other one.

NOBBY. A bite then.

MARY. I'm giving you a pound fifty. Don't lose it. (*Ushering him to the door:*) And don't linger.

NOBBY. I'm hungry.

MARY. Off you go.

NOBBY *is walking up the steep road on his own. He tries whistling to keep up his spirits.*

JASON (*far away*). Nobby. (*Whistles through his teeth.*) Nobby, wait.

NOBBY (*calling*). I can't.

JASON (*nearer*). Wait for me.

NOBBY. I gorra go t' Trotty's.

JASON *catches up with* NOBBY, *panting.*

JASON. Y' got yer conkers?

NOBBY. Aye.

JASON. I gorra great one here, it's a fiver. Could be a sixer.

NOBBY. She's taken them out me pocket. (*Anguished.*)

JASON. What?

NOBBY. Me mum's taken me conkers out me pocket.

JASON. I've got one here you can have.

NOBBY (*sighs*). I've gorra go t' Trotty's.

JASON. Jonathan gave me this one, look. It's got string through it and all. Take it, go on. Hold it out.

There is a smart crack as the conker splits. The lads yell lustily.

NOBBY. ⎱ Neh.
JASON. ⎰ Yeh.

JASON. I cracked it.

NOBBY. It's a bad one.

JASON. Keep it, I want the string.

NOBBY. I gorra go.

JASON. Where are you going?

NOBBY. I gorra go t' Trotty's.

JASON. I can come t' Trotty's with yer.

They make intermittent progress up the hill.

Y'can have me sixer if yer like. I got two sixers here. Take that one.

NOBBY. I'll have that one.

JASON. No, I want that one.

NOBBY. Go on, Jason, give me that one.

JASON. Go on then, hold it out.

NOBBY. You hold it out.

Gradually receding.

JASON. Don't hit too hard the first time.

NOBBY. Hold it still.

JASON. Don't hit too hard.

NOBBY. ⎱ YEH.
JASON. ⎰ NEH.

A dog barks far away.

MISS TROTTMAN *is crackling paper in her corner shop. A meandering conversation takes place.*

MISS TROTTMAN. Did I give you six ounces of bacon or was it a half, Mrs Peck?

MRS PECK. A half, weren't it, Miss Trottman?

MISS TROTTMAN. Let me weigh it again.

She does so.

And how much rice will it be, a pound?

MRS PECK. I'll take two. Nay, one'll do.

MISS TROTTMAN. Well, you've got that steep hill, haven't you, Mrs Peck?

MRS PECK. It's about time I got a basket wi' wheels.

MISS TROTTMAN. Oh, they're a saving grace. One pound of rice.

Rice is measured out.

Not yet six and look how dark it is outside.

MRS PECK. Is that the time? Look at me, I'm keeping you, Miss Trottman.

MISS TROTTMAN. No, I don't bother about the odd five minutes, Mrs Peck. (*Under her breath:*) Now let me see, that's sixty, sixty-five plus . . . That's a hundred and seventy-five plus forty . . . That's two pounds and seventy pence altogether, thank you, Mrs Peck.

The door bell clonks.

Oh, it's Nobby. Just in time, Nobby, I were about to lock up.

MRS PECK (*shrewdly*). You're a funny colour, Nobby Taylor.

Money is exchanged and the till clinks open.

MISS TROTTMAN. Thank you very much, Mrs Peck, and that's thirty-three pence change.

MRS PECK. That's it, Miss Trottman, thank you.

MISS TROTTMAN. Now, Nobby, what can I get for you?

A significant lack of response.

Well, what did you come in for? Did your mother give you a shopping list? Nobby, just think back to when your mother asked you to run up to the shop for her.

A lengthy pause.

Is it coming back? Oh, dear.

Sounds of a children's quiz show on television in GRANDAD's *room.*

MARY. Can you manage to get t' kitchen, Grandad? It's tea time. Stay there a minute. I'll turn this off.

The television switches off.

GRANDAD. I don't know if I can today. (*He winces.*) Eee, he has been playing me up.

MARY. Arthur?

GRANDAD. Aye, Arthur. Didn't know I were alive 'til he came a' visiting. Arthur bloody Itis.

MARY *sits.*

MARY (*gently*). Are you warm enough in here?

GRANDAD. 'Course I am. I keep an eagle eye on coal bucket.

MARY. It's rotten for you, Grandad. I should come in here to see you more often.

GRANDAD. Tha's busy, lass.

MARY. Aye, and what do I do with my time, what do I do? Nothing I can stand back and look at, any road.

GRANDAD. What are thee saying, Mary? Tha's keeping a family together.

MARY. Look at me, I don't stop shouting at you all from morning 'til night. What I'd like – is to be able to do something that only I could do. I'm talking daft, I can't say it properly.

A pause.

GRANDAD. What tha's done for me and Alice – nobody could 'a done better than thee, Mary. What tha's done for me and Alice – I'd like thee to know that us appreciates it.

MARY. Come on, tea time. Lean on me. Up, that's it. Here's your frame.

GRANDAD. Aye, aye, aye, aye. That'll do.

Fading.

MARY. We're waiting for Nobby to get back, he's gone t' Trotty's.

Sounds of footsteps labouring up the hill: MRS PECK's *and* NOBBY's

MRS PECK. You're my Good Samaritan, you are, Nobby. Can you manage?

NOBBY. Aye.

MRS PECK. You'd say if bag were too heavy for you?

NOBBY. No, it's all right.

An owl hoots.

MRS PECK (*draws her breath in through her teeth*). Hark at that owl, did you hear that, our Nobby? You can tell it's Halloween tonight.

Sounds of boiling water swirling into the teapot. Back in the kitchen.

MARY (*half to herself*). Where has that boy gone? I do not know what he gets up to. How long has he been gone, half an hour? It only takes five minutes to get up t' Trotty's and back. I don't know.

Striding to the door, opening it and calling.

Brian. Tea. Wake up. (*She closes the door.*)

GRANDAD. Come on, Mary.

MARY. Well, I don't know, Grandad – that boy . . . He's in a dream half the time. I should never have sent him out, look outside, it's almost dark. I blame myself. I blame myself.

GRANDAD. He'll be all right.

MARY. I might have known he'd take hours. Oh, God, when I think of what might have happened to him.

GRANDAD. Safe as houses round here.

MARY. It's no good, I've got to go and look for him. Where's my coat? Tell Brian when he comes down, to take . . .

GRANDAD. Just a ticket, just a ticket, that's him now.

The door opens.

NOBBY. I'm back, Mum.

GRANDAD. 'Course you are, lad, 'course you are.

MARY. I can see. Where have you been?

NOBBY. I had to take Mrs Peck's shopping up the hill for her.

MARY. That doesn't take half an hour.

NOBBY. She wouldn't walk very fast.

MARY. What have you got in that bag?

NOBBY. Bananas.

MARY. Why?

NOBBY. You told me to get them.

MARY. When?

NOBBY. From Trotty's.

MARY. I asked you to go up to Trotty's, but I never asked you to get bananas.

NOBBY (*weakly*). Yes yer did.

MARY (*on the brink*). When have I ever asked you to get bananas? I can't afford bananas.

GRANDAD. What's up, Mary?

MARY. We've only got no tea for tomorrow morning. Look what he's brought back with him. Bananas.

GRANDAD. I like a nice banana.

MARY. Take them back. Go on. Take them back t' Trotty's.

NOBBY. I can't, she's closed.

MARY. Well, knock on door.

NOBBY (*his voice rising*). I can't knock on door.

MARY. Why not, why can't you knock on door, she'll not mind.

NOBBY (*expecting instant extermination*). I've ate one.

Coal is being shovelled on to the fire from a long conical coal bucket.

GRANDAD. Gi' it a poke now.

BRIAN (*irritable*). Will you let me see to it.

GRANDAD. Aye, aye.

BRIAN. Just sit back and let me see to it. Gi' us poker.

> *He pokes the fire.*

> That'll come up now, gi' it a minute.

GRANDAD. Is Billy bringing terriers over tonight?

BRIAN. Aye, he'll be round affut meeting. He were talking to a bloke, Billy were, over Fellknapp way. Lost his terriers one night, this bloke, three of them. They found a hole, put terriers down. Didn't see them for a week.

GRANDAD. A week.

BRIAN. They thought it were a badger set, but it were bloody workings down there. Old workings. Poor little buggers. They was underground a full week, you know.

NOBBY. Mr Horne says you shouldn'a let dogs go after badgers.

BRIAN. 'Course you should, don't you know it's nature? You stop an animal from following its instincts, you make it unhappy. Same wi' us, and all.

NOBBY. Not if you love animals.

BRIAN. Nay, what are they doing, brainwashing you? You can't tell me this bloke don't love his animals, he took a week off work searching for them terriers. The wife and all. They were out there between them twenty-four hour a day. So don't you tell me he don't care for his animals.

> *The fire crackles and GRANDAD sighs.*

GRANDAD. Know what I'd give my life for now? A pint of Sam Smith's. All smooth and tangy.

> *The fire continues to burn. There is a slight rustle of dry leaves.*

NOBBY. What's that, Grandad, oak or ash?

GRANDAD. Oak or ash, that's beech, that is.

BRIAN. Looks like a leaf.

GRANDAD. Alice could tell thee, she were razor sharp on trees, summer and winter. Is that homework?

NOBBY. Aye.

GRANDAD. Identification?

NOBBY. No, I've got to say what leaf it is.

GRANDAD. Go up stairs and ask Gran, she don't make mistakes.

NOBBY (*wriggling uncomfortably*). No.

GRANDAD. Ah, Alice. (*Briskly:*) She'd like this fire, do her a world of good.

BRIAN. Aye well, doctor said she'd affut stop in bed for a couple of days.

GRANDAD. I don't like it, Brian. Did he not say why?

BRIAN. No, but give her time, she'll be up and about.

GRANDAD. I don't know. (*He ruminates.*) If I could just make it up stairs . . .

BRIAN. She's all right.

GRANDAD. She's missing me, I know she is.

BRIAN. Don't you believe it. She's having fantastic, fabulous dreams.

GRANDAD. Dreams?

BRIAN. Aye. Full of sex.

GRANDAD. Nay.

BRIAN. Oh, it's wicked what she's told me.

GRANDAD. Tell me.

BRIAN. Nude bathing.

> GRANDAD *tries to digest this.*

Topless aerobatics. Eh, it were terrible. I couldn'a listen in the end.

GRANDAD (*amused*). Not topless, though. She'd ne'er think of topless.

BRIAN. Don't count on it.

GRANDAD. Bye, tha's a bloody shamefaced liar. (*Vigorously:*) Puts me in mind of how she used to sport about in that swimming costume. What gaiety. Always. It's what counted, tha know, when times were hard.

BRIAN. When times were hard. Do you think life's a bloody holiday for us now?

GRANDAD. Tha's in work.

BRIAN. How long for?

GRANDAD (*suspicious*). What's that?

BRIAN. Closure.

GRANDAD. Never.

BRIAN. So they say.

GRANDAD. You've been up at 40 per cent these last three months.

BRIAN. Exactly.

GRANDAD. I can't believe it.

BRIAN (*irritated*). Don't you know we're a bloody backwater?

GRANDAD. There's enough coal in this earth under here to last us
for centuries. Centuries. This village could go on for ever. Nay
lad. Tha's not ready to lay down and die yet. Tha' mu'n fight on.
(*Almost beside himself.*)

BRIAN. It's rubbish, Grandad, the coal's rubbish. This village . . .
I reckon, in a year's time you'll be lucky to walk down street and
see a single living soul.

GRANDAD. Don't say it, don't say that.

BRIAN. Face up to it.

GRANDAD (*confidentially*). What about lad, eh? Have you thought
about it?

BRIAN. Thought about it. Look at him. Learning how to be a nature
lover. Just as well, i'nt it. There'll be nowt else left for him but
bloody nature.

GRANDAD. Fight, lad, fight.

BRIAN. It's people who fight. Statistics can't fight. The population
of this village can be divided up and packed off somewhere else,
no trouble at all, you just take a pencil don't you. Noughts
and crosses.

GRANDAD. I cannot fathom it, I cannot fathom it.

BRIAN (*briskly*). Aye well. We'll be thrashing all that out at meeting,
any road.

GRANDAD. Bye, I'd like to be there, Brian. I were a champion
platform speaker, you know.

BRIAN (*preparing to leave*). Tell you what, Grandad. I'll take you up to
see Gran when I come back.

GRANDAD (*brightening*). Will thee, lad?

BRIAN. Aye, later on.

NOBBY. T'ra, Dad.

BRIAN. You stay put. And there'll be no conkering from now on either.

The door opens and BRIAN *steps out into the hall.*

(*Calling:*) I'm off now.

MARY (*from upstairs*). Right, love.

MARY *is tucking* GRAN *in and straightening her bedclothes.*

You could do with an extra pillow, couldn't you, Gran?

GRAN. Who were that?

MARY. Brian, he's off t' meeting.

BRIAN (*from downstairs*). Back around eight or nine.

A distant door bangs.

GRAN. Did you say there were a meeting?

MARY. That's right.

GRAN. Is Norman going?

MARY (*fighting back the irritation*). No, you know very well, Grandad can't go. (*Kinder:*) It's cold outside, Gran. He's better off by fire.

GRAN. He used to come in wi' two pink dots on his cheeks . . .

MARY. Who?

GRAN. Norman.

MARY. When?

GRAN. After he'd been gassing at one of them meetings . . .

The door opens.

NOBBY. Grandad wants to go t' toilet.

MARY (*world-weary sigh*). Tell him I'm coming.

NOBBY. I'm going to see Jason now.

MARY (*surprised*). Well, have you finished your homework?

NOBBY (*evasively*). I can do it tomorrow if I want to.

MARY. Don't give me that, Nobby Taylor. You go straight downstairs and finish.

NOBBY. Can't find glue.

MARY. What do you want glue for?

NOBBY. I want it.

MARY. What for?

NOBBY. Leaves keep falling out.

MARY. Go on, I'm coming.

MARY *stacks* GRAN's *supper things on her tray.*

You'll be all right, Gran? I'm going up to see Miss Trottman now, I'll not be long. I'll send Nobby up with a cup of tea for you.

MARY *makes for the door.*

GRAN. There's nobody could have done more for me that what you have, Mary.

MARY *is dumbfounded.*

He's a grand lad, our Nobby.

MARY. Aye. He is.

MARY *has had a premonition:* GRAN *has never been known to notice what people do for her nor to pass a compliment. The door closes quietly.*

A rustling of dry leaves. Back in the kitchen.

NOBBY. I don't know how to do these leaves, Mum.

MARY *is pouring tea and trying to gather her thoughts together.*

MARY (*under her breath*). Last drop, just made it.

NOBBY. Mum.

MARY. Where have I put my purse?

NOBBY. I don't think this glue works, Mum.

MARY. I'm going mad, it's in my pocket.

NOBBY. It's not sticky.

MARY. No that's good, love, that's nice, I like it. Not too much glue. You can put that up on the wall when it's finished. After Mr Horne's seen it you can bring it home, can't you? It'd look nice on the wall up there.

NOBBY. I know what this is. A conker leaf.

MARY. Where did I put that bag of bananas?

NOBBY. Where are you going?

MARY (*picking up the paper bag*). I'm going t' Trotty's. I'll not be long. Take Gran's tea up for her, will you, love, she's waiting for it.

NOBBY (*whining*). No.

MARY. There you are, I've poured it out. Don't spill it now.

NOBBY. I don't want to.

MARY. I'll not be five minutes.

The door closes, the front door opens and bangs shut.
  A rattling of cup on saucer. A clumsy opening of GRAN's *bedroom door.*

NOBBY (*murmuring to himself*). Spilled some.

NOBBY *rattles perilously over to* GRAN's *bed and places the tea-cup on her table.*

(*Roughly like his father:*) Wake up, Gran.

A dead silence.

No, y' can't, y' can't. Don't die yet, Gran, me mum's gone out. (*Pause.*) She'll not be five minutes.

The television is playing in GRANDAD's *room. There is a knock on the door.*

GRANDAD. Who's that? Hang on a minute, let me switch this bugger off. (*With much effort he turns it off.*) Eh . . . that's better. Is that our Nobby?

NOBBY (*a small voice from the doorway*). Me mum's gone out.

GRANDAD. Has she lad? Come on in then, and close door behind you. (*Pause.*) Gone out, has she?

NOBBY. Aye.

GRANDAD. Taken bananas wi' her?

NOBBY. Aye.

GRANDAD. Great pity that. (*Pause.*) You've not smashed a plate, have you, lad?

NOBBY. No.

GRANDAD. Let kettle boil dry?

NOBBY. No.

GRANDAD. Tha's safe and dry then.

NOBBY. She gave me a cup of tea for Gran.

GRANDAD. Tha's not dropped it?

NOBBY. No.

GRANDAD. Well, I'm not going to bite thee, lad. See this? A dibbler. Know what a dibbler is?

NOBBY. No.

GRANDAD. It's for planting. You push it in t' earth and make a nice smooth hole. Then you take your cutting and dibble it in. Wilfred can have that, he'd appreciate it.

Silence.

Has tha' feet stuck t' floor? Not asleep, is she, your Gran?

NOBBY. No, her eyes were open.

GRANDAD. Taken her pills?

NOBBY. Don't know.

GRANDAD. Come on over here and give the fire a poke. Put more coal on it, that's it. Not too much, not too much or we'll both be in for it.

NOBBY *struggles with the coal bucket.*

NOBBY. It's gone out.

GRANDAD. Nay, it's not gone out.

NOBBY. It's gone all black.

GRANDAD. It'll come up again. Come and sit down here on stool and tell me about tha' poor old Gran. Did she have a bit of colour in her cheeks?

NOBBY. Don't know.

GRANDAD. What did she say to thee?

NOBBY (*panic*). She said, how's Grandad, Nobby?

GRANDAD. Did she now?

NOBBY. Aye. And she said, is he warm enough down there? And I said, aye, me mum's made a big fire for him.

The fire crackles into life.

GRANDAD (*delighted*). Sharp lad, tha's learning fast. Now look. Tonight, before tha' goes t' bed, I want thee to fill a hot water bottle and take it up for her. Use what's left in kettle. That clear? (*Pause.*) Saturday tomorrow. What have us got planned for tomorrow, our Nobby?

NOBBY. Don't know.

GRANDAD. Does tha' know what I think about sometime? Scarborough on a sunny Saturday. All them puffy little clouds and a great stretch of sand. Oh aye. Tha' gran looked quite something in them days. She had a fine chin, held it high. The wind blew her hat off one Saturday. Whipped it off her head and cartwheeled it across beach. Oh, it were miles before us caught up wi' it. But not before the wind had caught a hold of her hair. Her brown, long hair. I caught her by the waist and I said, Alice, I'm crazy about thee. And can thee guess what she said to me? 'I know!' Eee . . . That were a time when she could twist me round her little finger, tha' gran.

NOBBY. There were a fly on her face. She didn'a blink.

Silence.

A fly walked all over her nose, but she took no notice. She didn'a blink.

GRANDAD. What are thee saying, Nobby lad? A fly?

NOBBY. It walked all over her nose. Her eyes were open.

GRANDAD (*pause*). Did she not ask thee about me being warm enough and all that?

NOBBY (*faltering*). Not really, no.

GRANDAD. Tell me truly, Nobby lad, did she not say a word?

NOBBY. No.

GRANDAD. And thee put cuppa tea by her bed? Did she not move?

NOBBY. No.

GRANDAD. Not even to blink her eyes?

NOBBY. No.

GRANDAD. Alice. (*Acute regret:*) I were going to tell thee that I loved thee. Oh Alice. (*Controls his feelings.*) Good lad, our Nobby. Good lad.

A knocking at the front door.

NOBBY (*gasping*). Mum. That's me mum.

NOBBY runs to the door and opens it. There is a fraction's pause before a joyous pandemonium prevails. NOBBY's friends make all manner of ghostly sounds. NOBBY yells with terror and changes it to a laugh which he can't control.

EVERYBODY. Trick or treat?

RACHEL. Are you coming out, Nobby?

JONATHAN. Come on, Nobby.

JASON. It's great, we're scaring people.

JONATHAN. Aye, it's great.

NOBBY. I'm coming. I'm coming.

RACHEL. Ask your mum.

NOBBY. No, I can come, I can come.

JASON. We gorra pumpkin, and all.

JONATHAN. It's all lighted up.

JASON makes Tarzan's call of the jungle. The front door slams shut. Now NOBBY is outside with them, and they slowly wend their way down the road and away into the distance.

RACHEL. You can have my broom stick, if you like, Nobby.

1ST GIRL. He can have my hat.

JONATHAN. It's right scary out here. Shine torch on me face.

JASON. Eh, Nobby. Whoo . . . oooo.

   Much laughter from everybody, and a moment's lull.

RACHEL. Do you like me, Nobby?

LIFETIME

by Nigel D. Moffatt

Thanks to Acushla

Nigel D. Moffatt is a poet, musician, songwriter, playwright and writer. He was born in Jamaica in 1954. He came to England in 1961 and now resides in the West Midlands. In 1983 he recorded 'Peace, Love and Harmony' with Paul Weller. In the same year many of his poems were published in magazines. In 1984 he initiated a writer's group in Walsall. He has performed for many years in folk clubs. In 1985 he made his TV debut performing his own songs and poetry, and has continued to do so. Also in 1985 he was Writer in Residence at the National Theatre Studio, having *Tony* and *Rhapsody 'N Black 'N White* performed to an invited audience. *Tony* was subsequently staged by Sass Theatre Company at Oval House in 1987. His play *Mamma Decemba* (Birmingham Rep Studio, 1985, a joint production with Temba Theatre Company) won the Samuel Beckett Award and was published by Faber in 1987. In the same year he wrote *Keeping Walsall Boxed In* for Walsall LEA and West Midlands Arts Council with Common Ground. He is at present working on a new screenplay and stage play.

Lifetime was first broadcast on BBC Radio 4 on 26 May 1987, with Rudolph Walker as ARCHIE.

Director: Philip Marten
Running time, as broadcast: 29 minutes, 3 seconds

ARCHIE. Me have a lifetime of it! Lord! What a woman. Everything
  me do she a watch me. If she get up before me in the morning . . .
  she can't stand to know that me getting an extra hour and she on
  the staircase a hoover. If me shoulda get up before har; have me
  wash and dress meself; look in the mirror to comb me hair –
  whose eye me can feel burnin' out me backbone? She, yes. She
  think because she hidin' under the covers pretendin' to be asleep
  me don't know say she a watch me . . . but me know.
    She never miss a thing, make me tell you that. If me get up to
  go to the toilet, 'Where you goin'? Where you goin'?'. And me
  can't stay up there too long, either, me friend. 'What you a do up
  there for so long, you don't know you tea gettin' cold.'
    Some man go a toilet and stay up there for a hour . . . Me! Me
  don't even get time to wipe me arse. Me remember when me was
  at work, yu nuh, the man them used to take the *Sun* newspaper
  with them, when them go to the toilet . . . me never question
  them as to why . . . but them seem to enjoy the time them spend
  in there. Them come out happy you fart! Within a flash them
  gone down to the pub for a pint. Me used to feel sorry for them –
  thinkin' how lucky me was to be married to a woman like Marcy.
  Man, me was a damn fool!
    She never like pub, you see. A woman with a lot of pride, if you
  know what me mean. She don't go to the pub; she don't go to
  dance halls; she only eat chips if a she fry them; if it was for Marcy
  alone there would be no fish and chip shop in Britain. The only
  places she would go to was Church, and on special occasions
  when somebody we know from back home was gettin' married
  and we would go to the reception.
    Me suppose you coulda say me have less pride than Marcy; man,
  sometime me wouldn't mind if instead of the big pot a food on
  the fire, we could just walk down to the chip shop and get two
  bag a chip and a few piece of fish – me never was a big eater –

Marcy, she like har big pot a food, me friend.

Me wouldn't mind if now and again, like the white man them at work, we could go for a few drinks and to see some fresh faces. With Marcy a man need to see some new faces.

If me steppin' out of the house, 'Where you goin'? You nuh know say the pot on the fire? It nearly cook, yu nuh!' All me want to do is to go out and stretch me legs. If me go out before she cook . . . when me come back not a drop of food lef' for me. 'You expect me to cook for you while you out with some old hussy? You nuh see all the black man them who come a England with them nice, beautiful, black wife, lef' them for the little white hussy them you see them a walk pon street with – arm in arm – all the time.' And she go on, and on, and on, till har mouth get dry and she have to ask me if me want a cup of tea. A lifetime of it, me friend, a lifetime of it.

A so me work a week time, a so me give har me wage packet . . . without a thought, me friend. Me get me little spendin' money that she allow me for me tobacco; the rest go on food and house . . . something going safe every week into the bank.

She tell me when me need me hair cut; when me need new clothes; Man, me was never a fussy man. She would give me the exact amount to go and get me hair trim; the clothes me would get whilst out shoppin' with har on a Saturday mornin', that would quickly turn afternoon – you know how them can chat. Them meet one friend and them there all day – if you nuh say anything. There me would be, me two hands full with shopping bag, whilst Marcy choose the clothes she think me shoulda have.

'Don't put you big old dirty shoes on me new rug!' The time come, me friend, when me run out a patience. Me decide to act out a story one man did tell me a long time ago in Jamaica. Man, me say, me play mad! Me play mad! Me play mad 'til me me-self never know whether me was mad or not.

Me did have this little bag a yard that me used to use to take me sandwiches and flask a tea to work. Well, one mornin' me get up with the devil in a me. Me put two piece a clothes in there and take the bank book with me. Me go down town and draw out two hundred pounds. Then me come back. Well, by this time me did know that she woulda well mad – What!? Steppin' out the house with not even a bye or leave. Me walk all over har brand new rug – time and time again – then me go upstairs and find the money she thinks she was hidin' . . . a further two hundred pounds.

Me put it with the other two hundred me take out the bank and put it under the two piece a clothes at the bottom of the bag. Then me go downstairs and sit in the settee with the bag placed firmly in me lap . . . me didn't even take off me coat. 'Archie!' Same so she call me, 'What do you? You gone mad?' Up 'til now mad brother Archie don't answer har. Well, me friend, make me tell you; she call all har family down on me! brother, sister, uncle,

auntie . . . She even call har mother and father, but them never
come . . . because them dead long time ina Jamaica.

When the pressure hot up, me just take me-self and me bag and
walk out lef' all of them. One time them try to grab the bag away
from me – not the bag them want, yu nuh, make no mistake – a
the money inside there them was after. Me take out me little
penknife me used to carry to work with me . . . It make them
jump back, yu fart. From that them never trouble me. Marcy
calm down harself tu'. If me walk on har new rug a few times it
was all right, after all, what was a new rug compared to har very
valuable life? Them did think say me was dangerous, you see. Har
family tell har she should have me put away, but she never want
to know.

Me put the money back in the bank, and the other two hundred
pounds back upstairs. Me put away the old bag and take off the
old coat.

A week of pleasure me experience after that, me friend; but
that's as long as it did last. Har big eye them was on me again. She
never once talk bout when me was mad though, too afraid me
might go there again, you see.

Me used to work for Leyland one time, yu nuh; a there me meet
Sarah . . . one pretty little white girl, yu nuh. Well sa, a some of
the men there who introduce me to har; she smile with me and
was generally polite: me just think to me-self say she was a nice
girl. Man, next thing poor little old me know, the man them
come back sayin' how much the girl taken with me – how much
she want me to take har out. Me never know what to do with
me-self. A young girl like that wantin' to take up with an old bird
like me . . . Me couldn't understand that.

But when she come down on the factory floor, boy, and the
other man them a whistle, you fart fe see the girl eye them pon
me . . . me, yu nuh! Not anybody else . . . Oh. Sometime me
workin', she come stand by me and talk to me, ask me when me
goin' to take har for that drink me always been promising har.
Me never promise har no drink, yu nuh, but it did sweet a old
man to hear them words there coming from a young woman's lips.

The man them make a whole heap a noise when she look on me
or talk to me. Later them would come whisper to me bout how
me slow; 'It's there for the takin', Archie'; how she always askin'
them bout me; say she say she don't care if me married or not,
because that don't bother har – at least, not when it come to me.
Man, me was jumpin' from tree to tree, from limb to limb. Them
months there me never have much to do with Marcy, and at the
same time me can't say she did notice. She always said me was
never there.

Lord. This Sarah did sweet me at the time though. She give me
whole body a new lease of life . . . and me mean the whole of it.
When me see har me feel me temperature rise me say, man! Me

just have to laugh, yu nuh: an old bugger like me a fancy off young gyal. Me didn't even remember if me did know how to, or how not to . . .If me parts them still work . . . them work ina me head, but me didn't know about the old rusty body.

Man, at one point the girl was sayin' me promise to take har out for a drink, before you know it . . . me was promising to take the girl out for a drink. Next thing me know me was takin' off me overalls, goin' into the shower, then lookin' into the mirror to comb me hair, gettin' ready to meet har at the front gate. Man, me meet har, and meet har, and meet har again . . . and some good drink and laugh we have together tu'.

Marcy notice say me was openin' me pay packet, where as before me just used to take it go give har. Anyway, turn out this girl, Sarah, have a flat not too far from the pub – one of the Friday nights them she invite me back. Man, me fly like a bird . . . In there! Me float like a butterfly over the surface! Me sting like a bee and lef' me mark in there! Man, it was powerful! Me was alive again and dancing . . . something me could never do before.

Marcy notice say me was drinkin' on a Friday night, say she smell it on me breath . . . Man, she go mad. Me was comin' in much later, tu' . . . If drinkin' alone wasn't bad enough. She take me to see a private doctor, who, by the way, said me was in good health for a man of my age. Me thank him – in fact me end up thankin' the two of them . . . the doctor and Marcy.

Next thing, she find lipstick on me shirt – and she did know for certain it wasn't for har lipstick that lef' that mark. She go wild, Man! Then she start visitin' har sister six nights a week, after she serve me me dinner, when me come from work.

Now to put the icing on the cake, Sarah come a work come tell me say she pregnant, and a me responsible. Man, me take shame and guilt and go hide. The man them tease me bout how me goin' to tell me wife; when me goin' to tell me wife; what about when me wife find out and a nuh me tell har, but someone else.

Fear take me, me friend; fear take me over. Not one of them say 'if', not one. Panic strike me and me decide say if she goin' to know, me might as well make up me mind, and tell har me-self. Bam-kitty, me walk in the house the night, and who me buck upon . . . har lovin' sister, brother, uncle and aunt. Marcy was cryin' and her sister have har arm round har comfortin' har. Me first thought was that somebody dead . . . me couldn't guess who . . . but me know say a so them go on when somebody dead.

Man, when she see me she fling har big pot at me; cup; saucer; plate; you name it, boy, she fling it that night! Me have to run out me own house! And couldn't go in 'til night, when she was asleep, and har aunt, uncle, brother lef' the house – har sister sleepin' with har for the night. Me sleep in the spare room.

Four o'clock in the mornin' me wake, when me feel one hell of a fist rootin' out me rib-cage. It was Marcy standin' over me thumpin' me.

Still half asleep me couldn't believe what me was seein'. Har sister run into the room and parn har up, tellin' har she mustn't lower harself.

She found out, man; some busy-body tell somebody, who tell somebody else, who tell har sister, who tell Marcy. Man, life was unbearable for a long, long time. But you know, me did understand how she feel; it wasn't just due to me gettin' Sarah pregnant, you see, but you must understand that Marcy never have no children, and for her husband to have made another woman pregnant was more than she could bear.

One man at work explain it all to me. It all started out in fun, to see if me would react: go for a drink; behave as any normal male – normal as what them was used to. It turn out that most of the men them had passed through that dark tunnel at one time or another. Then she become pregnant. She tell them one by one, but them all just laugh at har – all that is, except old cunnu-munnu. So when me take charge them just carry on the joke. The man say them never did mean it to go so far, but things just get out of hand; then him apologise.

Me couldn't tell Marcy: to tell har would be to confront har with it again, and me would be admittin' openly – to har face – that me did do what she's been prayin' to God that me didn't do.

To this day she don't know a thing more or a thing less bout it.

Well, the girl lef' the factory. Me hear say she have the baby and she keep it. Me eyes never behold har again, me friend.

Five years later them make me redundant. After that, all me get is a little part-time job in one little dirty factory. All me do is collect scrap here and dump it there. Man, me never meet the likes of Sarah again; the closest me get is when the little factory girl them tease me, 'O'right old Archie?'. And then them tickle me ear or pinch me pon me chin. Me never too like it though, yu nuh.

For a year me do the little job, then them send come call me say because of cut-backs them have to sack me, and the job that me was doin' wasn't all that necessary when it come down to improvin' the productivity of the firm.

A the last job me ever have.

Me go home and work me little garden; plant me cabbage and potato. Marcy: 'Why you don't plant some nice flowers?' What I want to know is . . . can a man eat flowers when him hungry? A flowers we used to plant back home? Up 'til now . . . me don't answer har.

To this day me love me bit a gardenin', yu nuh. Sometimes me just pick up me-self and step out of the house, before Marcy even know say me put me coat on, me down the park. Me sit pon them little wooden bench and watch the ducks – and watch the little old white people them a feed them . . . Some of the old woman them used to look pon me and smile, yu see . . . me just smile back and tip me hat and go quietly on me way.

Me can sit for hours and don't know say hours pass when me in them garden . . . all kind of different flowers of all kind of different colours from all kind of different places . . . all of them there together a blossom.

Now, if me go tell Marcy this she goin' to want to know why me not growin' any flowers in we garden, so me just keep it quietly to me-self.

Me could sit here for hours and hours and hours . . . just watchin' them. Me don't know anything about flowers though! Don't misunderstand me . . . me just like the look of them. Fresh, alive, not witherin' like me-self ya.

Ay, boy. Marcy sick with high blood pressure and diabetes; doctor say she too fat and must lose weight, but she keep on cookin' har big pot a food them. Me tell har! But Marcy is not a woman to listen to anyone – about anything – at any time. As for me now, me just sick . . . sick of the cold; sick of England; home-sick . . . Man, me just sick. Sick of being old when me mind feel so young. Sick of havin' so much time and nothin' to do with it.

An old grey-head man like me-self should be sittin', or workin', out in the sun: and when me dead, me dead: but at least me woulda dead a happy old man – with a grin pon me face.

Me never get to go back, no, only Marcy . . . Marcy and har sister. Man, me not even been to Blackpool and see the lights, whatless go back home.

Me hear English people talk about goin' pon holiday, but that's all me know about this 'holiday'.

Me learn to content me-self with what me have, early on in life. Me father, me never know; me mother, a honest and Christian woman, dead before me even marry Marcy . . . and me and Marcy married fifty years now . . . and me is only seventy. Me know me don't look it – but me's only seventy. Me one brother get shot in Kingston and dead; me one sister go live with one man at fifteen . . . the last me hear of har she in America as wife to the man . . . don't ask me what that mean, because me don't know. All me know is she livin' in America . . . wherever that is.

Man, nobody did want to know me after me mother dead! Me one! Me one alone, me tell you . . . have to find money to bury har and money to buy drink and food as is we custom when anybody dead.

People come drink the drink; laugh them laugh; eat the food; all them say is, 'Boy, yu mother dead? Lord, but yu give har a good sendin' off though'. When them eat off the food done and drink off the drink, them gone. Me one, me a tell yu, me friend.

When Marcy father dead and har relatives – near and far – start to go a England, that a when all the trouble start. We must go to England tu'.

So, we sell up shop and come a England. All har relatives live side by side – or so it seemed to me at the time.

But me did think say me come a long, long way, and me was lucky to be where me was. Me start off with nothin', and end up with something, so me wasn't about to complain. We live good, eat when we want to, buy and save more or less when we want to. No, sa, not me . . . me never have a thing to complain about.

Sunday mornin's we get up early to get ready for church. Man, if me have on the wrong tie or the right tie, me don't know . . . the woman come after me, 'A that tie you wearin' to church? A the only tie you have? You want people think we a pauper? And look pon you shirt! You want people think say me don't look after you?' For the sake of some peace me just shut me mouth and go change the tie and shirt. 'A that jacket you goin' to wear with that tie and shirt?' She can't change and me can bear it, so me just go along with it.

A when me was at church me meet Benjamin and him wife Miss Pam – so people call har – but me just call har Pam. Man, from we met, we get on. Only five years in we age.

When me buck up on them ina church – anywhere we deh – Pam run come parn me and give me one breed a kiss, yu see; Benjamin fling him hand round me and give me one hug, yu see . . . Man, them never give a damn what people think or what people want to say. See them walking down the street holdin' hands like any young teenager. Sometimes me see them with them bag of fish and chips, one deh steal the chip out the other one bag.

Man, me say it sweet me, it sweet me, it sweet me 'til me can't tell you how much it sweet me. Them would even give me one bag of the chips and them share the other. Me eat it . . . and enjoy it tu'. Lick me finger afterwards you fart. If Marcy know . . . she kill me! But me didn't give a damn, me-self. Them make me feel good man! Like a new man! It was good and me enjoy it. Me spend hours and hours with them . . . me even spend half a day with them a few times. When me come back now, Marcy don't cook any dinner for me. The food never bother me, me was use to har ways by now; me have dinner and a snack when me out. Sometimes me already have me bag of fish and chips – lick me finger – before me come home.

Me did like the way Pam was with Benjamin, Man; just easy goin', takin' things easy. If Marcy was like that . . . we woulda move mountain! Instead, she just a jump and a kick like a wild horse; no time to enjoy anything, except cookin' har big pot a food.

Well sa, me, Benjamin and Pam gettin' on like a house on fire – when bam! Somebody tell somebody, who tell somebody, who tell her sister, who tell she . . . Marcy, say Pam was nothin' but a old tramp when them know har back home.

Them say she married four times before she buck upon

Benjamin, and all the man them old enough to be har pa. One by one them all dead off, leaving har everything; people in the district say she obeah them, or she sweat life out a them . . . Yes, same thing me did think, but a same so them tell me, 'She sweat life out a them'. Them say after the last husband, the family of the dead man, who never get anything from him will, run har out the district. She go to Kingston go live for a year then she come back with Benjamin, who help har settle up har business affairs there, then them lef' and come a England. Them say she have three picny over there, all a them she lef' with har old mother. People say she never even write to them or har mother since she come a England.

Marcy say me must have something goin' on with har that's why me won't stop goin' up there. Me could see in har eye she was thinkin' of what did happen between me and Sarah.

Well, me friend, me stop goin' up there for a while, and after that, just once in a while. Within a few week of me hearin' the gossip; them stop comin' to church. When me go up there again . . . Man, everything different. Not the same two people me used to run joke and have a laugh with. Them draw into themself. When me go up them used to try, but me could see that's all it was.

Me see up close what them tongue do to Pam and Benjamin . . . it destroy them! Them drag them down to them own level . . . and God knows that's no place to be.

Sometime we in a town a do we little shoppin' we would buck upon them. 'Come on!' is the first thing that come out of Marcy mouth . . . and in a second she gone. Me stop and have a little chat with them, but them never say much. Man, them look thin! Worry was killin' them.

Overnight, tongues change them love into hatred and bitterness . . . them didn't know whether them was comin' or goin' . . . them so confuse.

Benjamin did long give up on life, when me hear say him dead. 'Poor man', a same so Marcy say. It never come as no surprise to me as me did know the same feelin' him did have, for many, many more years than him. The man give up on life, Man.

You want to see the johncrow them gather at Pam's house . . . Man, it put me in mind of when me mother dead. The same people who talk them, a the very same people gather in the house to see what them can steal; eat; drink; what them can learn so them can talk for months later behind har back. Well, sa, me befriend the woman in har time of need, and that is all – under God's roof – that's all me was guilty of. No sooner Benjamin body under ground them start talk say a Pam kill him. Them say she go to London to one obeah man and she come back with something to put in him drink and a so him come to dead. Them say she did want all them have for harself, as Benjamin did find out har game, and it's from there him first take sick. Them say she did want another man – wait for it! And the other man was me . . . me say sa, me couldn't do nothin' better than laugh. Marcy never laugh. She take it to heart and before me know it she in hospital. She never in there for long before them let har out; while she in there Pam take a overdose of sleepin' tablets the doctor did give har after Benjamin dead; she go into the hospital, but the only place she come out to was a dark hole six foot underground, to lie on top of Benjamin . . . the dirt still soft and the wreaths still on top of the grave from when Benjamin bury.

'You see what happen now?' Man, can't miss a thing with Marcy around. 'You see how far you name go in a it?' She was off and gone! She was on fire, man! 'Look how long we in this country and nobody have a bad name to give we 'til you meet these damn bush people. Me come from a respectable family, me never grow a bush like a yu! Now look what you do to we name.' So me look, but me never see not'n'. 'Where would you be without me, tell me that? Lord have mercy, this blasted man who couldn't even read or write, me pick him up, marry him, and now see the ingratitude!' Me could only write me name then, and still me can only write me name now. Me never tell har that, though.

Doctor say har heart don't too good and she must take things easy, cut down on greasy food . . . and lose some weight. Marcy just carry on the same way . . . cookin' har big pot a food them and makin' enough noise to drill the whole of the British Army.

She believe all what people say to har and believe say them believe what she say to them – me, me just keep me mouth shut and mind me own business. Me see enough people who come a England around the same time as we, dead off one by one – and for what?

Me old now, all me want is some peace and quiet, time to ready me-self for what soon come.

Time . . . so precious, yu nuh. You don't notice till you only have a little of it. Man, you no sooner young – you old – grey and wrinkle with no time.

You live you life with other people, but really you live you whole life inside yu-self. You think of yu-self, what you want to do, and you love and hate just the same.

Time is the most precious thing a person can give, yu nuh. That's how love come to form – or hate – the two of them come the very same way. Take Benjamin and Pam before the tongue them mash up them life. Them give each other them time, that's what did make them different, make them so happy and easy goin'. Me never learn that 'til it was too late. Too late now.

Not much happen this time of the day, yu nuh, it go quiet in the afternoon.

House empty, nobody to talk to, just them damn bills and more bills; what for me don't know, because I don't understand them.

Man, me never there! Me only sleep there! So what bills can
I have to pay? Me just throw them in the bin.

Me come here and sit down sometime, yu nuh, in the exact,
same place me was sittin', when them call me to tell me say,
Marcy dead.

All she wanted was some attention from me; some of me time.
Now me dress in me coat and carry me little bag everywhere me
go: all me have to show for a whole lifetime.

LANGUAGES SPOKEN HERE

by Richard Nelson

Richard Nelson is the author of *Principia Scriptoriae* which was presented in 1987 by the Royal Shakespeare Company, directed by David Jones, and by the Manhattan Theatre Club in New York and *Between East and West*, produced in 1988 at The Hampstead Theatre Club. Other plays which include *The Vienna Notes*, *Rip Van Winkle* or *The Works*, *An American Comedy* and *The Return of Pinocchio* have been produced by many theatres in the United States. Nelson's adaptation and translations (including *The Suicide*, *Three Sisters*, *The Marriage of Figaro* and *Don Juan*) have been seen at theatres across the United States and on Broadway. Nelson is the recipient of a 1987 Time Out Award, two Obie Awards, a Guggenheim Fellowship, the 1986 ABC Television Playwriting Award, two Rockefeller Grants for playwriting and two National Endowment for the Arts writing fellowships, including the first two-year grant given.

Languages Spoken Here was first broadcast on BBC Radio 3 on 11 December 1987. The cast was as follows:

MICHAEL MILICK, *late thirties, American, translator from German and now Polish*	Colin Stinton
ANNIE MILICK, *thirties, British, Michael's wife, and assistant to Carol Howard, Michael's literary agent*	Emily Richard
JANUSZ VUKOVSKI, *fifties, Polish, novelist, playwright*	Renny Krupinski
JAN KOSKTA, *early forties, Czech writer, he speaks no English*	Jiri Hanak
ANDREW, *thirties, producer of a small theatre, British*	Peter Craze
GEORGE SIMPSON, *thirties, British, involved in publishing*	Steven Harrold
PETER MACK, *forties, British, involved in publishing*	John Samson
JANE, *thirties, British, involved in publishing*	Karen Archer

Time and place: today, London

Director: Ned Chaillet
Running time, as broadcast: 62 minutes, 57 seconds

1 Michael and Janusz meet

Interior. JANUSZ's flat. Morning. Door buzzer. JANUSZ's footsteps as he goes to the door. He opens the door..

MICHAEL. Mr Vukovski?

JANUSZ. Yes.

> *A short pause.*

MICHAEL. Mr Janusz Vukovski?

JANUSZ. What do you want?

MICHAEL. Michael. Michael Milick.

JANUSZ. Yes.

> *Beat.*

> I thought you said nine. Come in.

> *Footsteps.*

MICHAEL. No, ten. I even wrote down 'ten'. You haven't been waiting since nine, I hope, Mr Vuk . . .

JANUSZ. Janusz. Call me Janusz.

> *Beat.*

> This is the West, after all. How do you do?

MICHAEL. I'm sure we said . . . .

JANUSZ. Some tea?

MICHAEL. I'm never late. I'm practically famous for never being . . . .

JANUSZ. Or is it coffee?

> *A short pause.*

MICHAEL. Tea.

Beat.

If it's no trouble.

JANUSZ. Why should tea be trouble?

Beat.

I have a kettle.

JANUSZ *turns on the tap and fills the kettle.*

(*As he fills it:*) The first object I buy. I also have biscuits. And I am soon going to buy also a little cart to pull my groceries in.

He finishes with the tap.

There is not much more to being British that I can see. Don't you agree?

MICHAEL. I don't know. I'm American.

JANUSZ. This I know.

Beat.

It was my thought that you and I could make jokes of the British together.

Beat.

When I am with a British person, we have no problem making fun of the Americans.

Beat.

Did you know this?

MICHAEL. I'm not surprised.

Beat.

JANUSZ. What I do not understand though is why when the Americans and the British get together you never make jokes about the Polish.

Beat.

You never do this, do you?

Beat.

I have been told this many, many times.

MICHAEL (*laughs to himself*). To be honest . . . .

JANUSZ. Please don't tell me this isn't the truth. I could not bear to think I have been lied to by my new friends. I put so much trust in them.

Beat.

I have no choice but to trust them.

Beat.

And that is the only way to trust. When you have no choice. Don't you agree?

MICHAEL (*after a short pause*). I don't know.

JANUSZ. Please, eat a biscuit. I bought them for you.

A short pause.

Take another one.

Beat.

Take a third one.

MICHAEL (*with his mouth full*). No, thank you.

JANUSZ. This morning, at the Sainsbury's . . . and what a shop that is; the size!

MICHAEL (*mouth full*). By American standards . . . .

JANUSZ. I was there buying these biscuits to have for you, and I say to myself . . . this Mr Milick . . . .

MICHAEL (*mouth full*). Michael.

JANUSZ. Michael.

Beat.

Thank you, Michael. Thank you.

Beat.

I want him . . . you . . . to like me. Not only my novel which I know he will like . . . .

Beat.

And want to translate.

Beat.

But also me. (*He laughs.*) Two months in the West and already I am full of anxieties. (*He laughs.*)

Pause.

So I think I shall bribe you with biscuits. But you are not bribed, are you?

MICHAEL. I don't think so.

JANUSZ. Then allow me to tell you how very lucky I am to have caught your attention, Michael. Everyone has told me this. Everyone speaks like this about you.

MICHAEL. I'm flattered.

JANUSZ. This is the intention.

Pause.

You have not read my book?

MICHAEL. No. But I assumed . . . or presumed . . . that this was one of the reasons for my coming by.

Beat.

To pick up a copy.

JANUSZ. In Poland it is a very well-known book.

MICHAEL. I understand that. I'm eager to read it.

JANUSZ. Not that there aren't better books. Two of my books are better than this.

Beat.

And three of my plays. I have plays as well.

A short pause.

Successful plays.

The kettle boils.

There is your tea.

MICHAEL. You're not having any?

The kettle stops boiling.

JANUSZ. Sit down, please. This is the comfortable chair. This one is not broken yet. (*As he serves the tea:*) I suppose it wouldn't take long to read the book. It is rather a short book.

MICHAEL. I plan to read it right away.

JANUSZ. One could read it in one night, I suppose.

A short pause.

MICHAEL. I couldn't tonight.

Beat.

If that's what you're . . . .

JANUSZ. Milk?

MICHAEL. Yes.

A short pause.

I'm busy tonight. Maybe tomorrow though.

Beat.

Tomorrow isn't too late, is it?

JANUSZ. Tomorrow? No.

Beat.

Why would tomorrow be too late? Ten o'clock wasn't too late.

MICHAEL. Really, I'm pretty positive I said . . . .

JANUSZ. Nine. Ten. Today. Tomorrow.

Beat.

Next year.

Beat.

So I wait. I have nothing else to do.

Beat.

What are you doing tonight that makes you so busy?

MICHAEL. A meeting.

Beat.

A party.

Beat.

With a lot of publishing types.

JANUSZ. That is important for a translator? To be with publishing types?

MICHAEL. I'm told so.

A short pause.

JANUSZ. And for writers too it must be a good thing . . . to meet publishing types.

Beat.

No?

MICHAEL. Yes. I would think so.

JANUSZ. I have met very few people here. Is there a special purpose for this party?

MICHAEL. No purpose. Just to get together.

Beat.

And talk.

Beat.

Put faces to names.

A short pause.

Janusz I'd ask you to come along, but I hardly know the other . . . .

JANUSZ. I would be in the way.

MICHAEL. No, it's not . . . .

JANUSZ. I wasn't asking to come.

MICHAEL. I now you weren't, but . . . .

JANUSZ. Anyway, I see my friend, Jan Kostka, tonight.

Beat.

You know my friend, Jan Kostka?

MICHAEL. No. I don't think I . . . .

JANUSZ. We get together and praise each other's books. He loves my books. I didn't think a Czech would like them so much.

Beat.

His books are not so good. But I don't tell him, of course.

A short pause.

He is a very good friend. He visited me once in Warsaw. He saw what a big flat I had there.

Pause.

Where did you study Polish?

MICHAEL. I am Polish. Didn't my agent tell you?

JANUSZ (*in Polish*). *From where?*

MICHAEL (*in English*). Hamtramack, Michigan.

JANUSZ (*in Polish*). *Where?*

MICHAEL (*English*). Michigan. That's in the Midwest. It's a state.

Beat.

Some of it is very Polish.

Beat.

There's even a Mass in Polish in Hamtramack.

A short pause.

I took my degree though in German. And it's mostly German that I . . . .

JANUSZ (*in Polish*). *How's the tea?*

MICHAEL (*English*). The tea is fine, thank you.

A short pause.

JANUSZ (*in Polish*). *Another biscuit, Michael?*

MICHAEL (*English*). Two biscuits are plenty, thanks.

A short pause.

If this is a test, I do read it quite fluently.

Pause.

Though I've mostly translated from the German.

JANUSZ. Yes?

MICHAEL. Let me give you a list of my titles. Here's a list. There.

A short pause.

JANUSZ. Well.

MICHAEL. Didn't my agent give you the list?

JANUSZ. Yes.

Beat.

Yes, she did. (*He chews a biscuit.*) I cannot wait to know what you think of my book, Michael. I shall be so interested to talk to you about it.

Beat.

Someone who knows Polish. Someone who is . . . 'Polish'. This is very exciting for me.

A short pause.

Tomorrow morning I shall sit myself down next to that phone, Michael.

MICHAEL. Janusz . . . .

JANUSZ. First thing in the morning, I shall do this.

MICHAEL. Now you know I may not even get to it until the early afternoon.

JANUSZ. Michael, I have nothing else to do.

Beat.

Nothing. What do I have to do?

Beat.

But wait for you.

Fade out.

2 Learning to play

Interior. A flat in Islington. Early evening. A party is going on: loud talk, music, etc.

GEORGE (*over the music*). Michael, would you be a dear and reach me one of those white wines?

Beat.

Thanks.

Beat.

You're not drinking?

MICHAEL. I have reading to do tonight.

GEORGE. You *are* conscientious.

MICHAEL. That's why I can't stay . . .

JANE. George, is that you?

GEORGE. Jane.

JANE. Have you two met?

PETER. I don't believe . . .

JANE. Peter Mack, George Simpson.

GEORGE. Oh, Peter Mack. (*He recognises the name.*) How do you do?

PETER. How do you do?

GEORGE. And this is Michael Milick.

OTHERS. Hello. Hello.

MICHAEL. Hello.

JANE. American?

MICHAEL. Yes.

PETER. You can tell from one 'hello?'

JANE. Can't you?

GEORGE. Michael's been here for years now, or so he's been telling me.

PETER. Then we won't have to worry about him starting to act American.

JANE. How long is 'for years?'

MICHAEL. Nearly five now. I figure five more and you'll have me civilised.

They laugh.

OTHERS. Cheers.

MICHAEL. Sorry, I don't have a glass.

ANNIE (*coming up to* MICHAEL). Michael, did Carol find you? She was looking for you. Excuse me.

MICHAEL. This is George. This is . . .

JANE. Jane.

MICHAEL. Jane. This is Peter Mack. My wife, Annie.

OTHERS. How do you do?

PETER. Have we met?

ANNIE. I work for Carol Howard.

PETER. Of course.

GEORGE. And married to an American? We let you girls do that, do we?

JANE. Are you an agent then too, Michael?

MICHAEL. No. Carol Howard's *my* agent. I translate.

PETER. Into American? (*He laughs.*)

ANNIE. No, from German.

MICHAEL. And now maybe from Polish. I'm about to start working on a novel by Janusz Vukovski. Do you know him?

JANE. Janusz Vuk . . .

MICHAEL. Vukovski.

JANE. Those Polish names.

PETER. Never heard of him.

The music gets louder.

MICHAEL. He's very well known in Poland.

GEORGE. And as Poland goes . . . (*He laughs.*)

MICHAEL (*trying to speak over the music*). Two or three of his books have done very well in French.

ANNIE. And also in Italian. Carol thinks . . .

JANE. Who's the publisher?

MICHAEL. Here?

JANE. Yes, in London.

MICHAEL. There isn't one yet.

JANE. Ah. But there soon will be, won't there?

ANNIE. We're sure of it.

MICHAEL. Actually, Mr Mack, perhaps when I get a few chapters done, one of your editors could . . .

Music loud.

PETER. What? I can't . . .

MICHAEL. I think he's one of the most important Eastern European novelists today!

PETER (*having to almost shout now over the music*). Who?

MICHAEL. Vukovski!

ANNIE. He's sort of like a Polish Norman Mailer, Mr Mack!

A short pause. Loud music.

MICHAEL. Or a Polish John Le Carré!

Cut out.

3 A favour is done

Interior. MICHAEL *and* ANNIE'*s flat in Chiswick: the bedroom and*
bathroom. Night. Footsteps. The bathroom light is switched on. MICHAEL
begins to brush his teeth.
   Pause.

ANNIE. Well, how is it?

MICHAEL. I thought you were asleep.

ANNIE. I was. How is it?

MICHAEL. I'm sorry if I woke . . .

ANNIE. Michael, how's the bloody book? I've been sitting on pins.

MICHAEL. You were asleep sitting on . . .?
   Beat.
   It's good, Annie. It is good.

ANNIE. Thank God.
   Beat.
   It is Good.
   Beat.
   Now I'll go back to sleep.

MICHAEL. I like it a whole lot.
   Beat.
   It's pretty damn good.
   A short pause.

ANNIE. *Pretty* damn good?
   A short pause.

MICHAEL. I don't know. Maybe I shouldn't have read it at night.

ANNIE. Oh Christ, it's bad.

MICHAEL. It's not bad.
   Beat.
   It is not bad.
   Pause.
   It's about a guy who's lost most of his hair. And so he goes out
   and buys this hairpiece which he only puts on when he goes to
   bed with his wife.
   Beat.
   He goes to bed with a lot of other women. But he only wears the

hairpiece for his wife.

Pause.

ANNIE. That's it?

Beat.

It's bad. Shit.

MICHAEL. That's the basic thing, yeh. I mean he . . . the guy . . .
goes through a lot, but that is what it keeps coming back to.
Screwing his wife while wearing a hairpiece.

Beat.

To be honest I don't get it.

ANNIE. Must be some sort of metaphor.

MICHAEL. Yeh.

Beat.

So?

Pause.

It's short at least . . . not even two hundred pages.

ANNIE. Michael, if it's no good . . .

MICHAEL. Annie, I liked him!

Pause.

You should see where he lives.

ANNIE. You told me.

MICHAEL. I *have* heard of him, Annie. In Poland he is somebody.

Beat.

His whole flat could fit in here in our bedroom.

Beat.

If I turned him down . . .

ANNIE. What? What awful thing would happen?

MICHAEL. I don't know.

A short pause.

I called Carol. Just before I finished tonight. I wanted to know
more about him.

Beat.

She said he's got a wife and three kids he's trying to get out.

ANNIE. And live on what?

MICHAEL. This book I suppose.

ANNIE. Oh God.

Pause.

MICHAEL. Well, it is not all that terrible. There are some quite funny parts.

Beat.

Some amusing bits.

A short pause.

Who knows, maybe there's a chance of actually getting it published. I can talk to John at Faber's. Maybe he can slip it by.

A short pause.

Though I think we can forget Peter Mack.

ANNIE. Yes.

A short pause.

MICHAEL. I mean, what is the worst that can happen?

Beat.

I'll be practicing my Polish.

Beat.

I'll be spending some time getting to know Janusz. I'm sure that'll be a hoot.

Beat.

When you think what it means to . . .

A short pause.

Hell, Annie, what's to lose?

Fade out.

4 Tea and biscuits given again

Interior. JANUSZ's *flat. Day.*

JANUSZ (*reads*). 'The Bald Spot by Janusz Vukovski.'

Beat.

This is a good title?

MICHAEL. It's your title, Janusz.

Beat.

Basically.

JANUSZ. Excuse me, I was getting you a plate for the biscuits . . .

MICHAEL. I'm really fine like . . .

A short pause.

'Treska' means 'bald spot', Janusz.

Beat.

Technically . . . literally . . . of course, it means what? 'Hairpiece', 'toupee'. But . . .

A short pause.

Believe me, '*The Bald Spot*' is a terrific title for the book. Sounds very . . .

Beat.

It's very European. *Eastern* European.

Beat.

Annie thinks so too.

JANUSZ. Annie?

MICHAEL. My wife.

JANUSZ. Of course. We haven't met.

MICHAEL. No. She loves the title.

Beat.

She's English.

JANUSZ. Then she ought to know.

Pause.

MICHAEL. Annie even said . . .

The kettle boils.

JANUSZ. I'm sorry.

He goes to the kettle. It stops boiling.

MICHAEL. Annie said . . . She was imagining, you know, an older British couple walking down the road, one turns to the other and says . . . 'Oh Robert, look in the window of that bookshop. *The Hairpiece*, now there's a book I'd like to curl up with. (*He laughs.*) '*The Hairpiece.*' (*He laughs.*) Ridiculous, isn't it, when it's translated. It sounds . . . (*He laughs.*) You see what I mean. Why we needed to make it '*The Bald Spot*'.

Pause.

JANUSZ. Here's your tea, Michael.

Pause.

(*He reads.*) '*The Bald Spot* by Janusz Vukovski.' (*He sits in a very creaky chair.*) This week I shall buy another chair that is not broken.

MICHAEL. Please, sit . . .

JANUSZ. No, no.

Pause. The chair creaks.

MICHAEL. You don't have to read what I've done now. I could come back . . .

A short pause.

JANUSZ. I am sorry, I read English very very slowly.

MICHAEL. That's OK. Look, I'll come back tomorrow.

Beat.

You should take your time.

Beat.

I'll keep working. I don't think I'm too far off with those first ten pages.

Beat.

Style . . . that's what I'm most nervous about.

Beat.

If I've gotten the style right.

Beat.

Close enough.

Pause.

I'll finish my tea and leave you alone then.

Beat.

And come back. Tomorrow?

JANUSZ. '*The Bald Spot.*' Yes.

Beat.

Our Minister of Defence wears a hairpiece.

Beat.

In Poland . . . in Warsaw, you say 'hairpiece' and everyone thinks . . . 'Minister of Defence'.

Beat.

I don't suppose you do here.

MICHAEL. What? Think 'Polish Minister of Defence' when we hear 'hairpiece?'

JANUSZ. Yes.

MICHAEL. No. (*He laughs lightly to himself.*) We don't think that.

Beat.

I don't.

Beat.

I can guarantee you that.

Pause. JANUSZ *creaks in the chair.*

Janusz, you mean, it's a reference then? The title?

Beat.

To the Polish Minister of Defence?

A short pause.

JANUSZ. Please, eat a biscuit. I bought this whole new package just for you.

Fade out.

5 Michael gives a dinner and chairs

Interior. MICHAEL *and* ANNIE's *flat. Evening.*
  Footsteps up the stairs.

MICHAEL (*calls back down into the cellar*). I'll be right back down, Janusz!

Beat.

(*Quietly:*) What do you think . . . should we ask him to stay for dinner?

Beat.

We can get Indian.

ANNIE. I might have a chicken.

MICHAEL. Whatever. I just think he'd like it. God knows how he feeds himself. He doesn't even have a kitchen.

ANNIE. I'll see what I need. (*She starts to walk away.*) Michael?

MICHAEL. What?

ANNIE. I like him. I really do.

Beat.

I see what you mean.

MICHAEL. He's a fascinating bugger, isn't he? I better go back down and see what he's found. (*As he goes back down the cellar steps.*) Find one you want, Janusz?

JANUSZ (*in the cellar*). I think it is between two.

MICHAEL. Then take them both if you want.

JANUSZ. No. No, I don't think I . . .

MICHAEL. Janusz, we have never even used either one of those chairs. They've been down here since Annie's mother died.

Beat.

Take them. Please.

Beat.

It's you who'll be doing us a favour.

A short pause. MICHAEL *coughs.*

It's really dusty down here.

Beat.

Come over here, I think there's a lamp you might like . . .

Footsteps. Fade out. Cut to: the dining-room, MICHAEL, ANNIE *and* JANUSZ *in the middle of dinner.*

More potatoes?

JANUSZ. Thank you. Yes.

Beat.

So the last I hear is my wife and two of the children can leave, but the third child, she will have to stay with my mother-in-law.

ANNIE. They can do that?

JANUSZ. Of course, yes.

ANNIE. But that's like kidnapping, Michael.

JANUSZ. It is not that I do not like my mother-in-law . . .

ANNIE. No, no.

MICHAEL. That's not what Annie thought.

ANNIE. No.

JANUSZ. She still teaches in the school. Seventy-two years old.

Beat.

Alzhbeta is ten.

MICHAEL. She's the one who would have to stay behind?

JANUSZ. Yes. She's the youngest.

Pause. They eat.

ANNIE. Janusz, if there is anything that we . . . Michael and I . . . can . . .

Beat.

Michael?

MICHAEL. I don't know what, Annie.

JANUSZ. Please. Please.

Beat.

But I thank you.

A short pause.

Anyway, my wife says she will wait until they can all leave
together. This is what she says today.

Beat.

In her last letter.

Beat.

Either wait for this. Or I should come back.

MICHAEL. Is that a real possibility? Your going back?

Pause.

JANUSZ. Delicious chicken, Annie.

ANNIE. Thank you.

A short pause.

MICHAEL. I'll open another bottle of wine.

Pause.

ANNIE. Michael? I was just thinking, you know Father's cottage in
East Sussex?

Beat.

No one ever goes there anymore.

MICHAEL. You mean for Janusz?

JANUSZ. No, no, please!

ANNIE. To use when you wanted. Not to move there.

JANUSZ. Of course, I didn't think . . .

MICHAEL. It's in a beautiful spot.

ANNIE. Gorgeous! Incredibly quiet.

JANUSZ. Really, I don't . . .

MICHAEL. After dinner we'll show you some photos . . .

ANNIE. The truth is, you'd be doing us the favour.

JANUSZ. Thank you.

Beat.

Thanks.

Pause. They eat.

So tell me, Michael, does one finally adjust to someone else's country after five years?

MICHAEL. You mean me?

ANNIE. I think Michael's adjusted remarkably well.

MICHAEL. You think so?

ANNIE. I do. I really do.

MICHAEL. It wasn't that hard. The people are nice.

A short pause.
  He pours wine. Pause.

But I'm not saying there aren't things about the States that I miss. You've never been, right?

JANUSZ. No.

MICHAEL. Neither has Annie, but we're hoping to fix that, aren't we?

ANNIE. We'll see, Michael.

Beat.

Let's see.

MICHAEL. Michigan is a very beautiful state. It's one of the states that has everything. Big cities. Big beaches. Farms. Lakes. The Upper Peninsula is . . . Well, I'm not sure they even let cars in some places. It is that spectacular.

Beat.

That's where Hemingway spent a lot of his time.

JANUSZ. I thought that was Cuba.

MICHAEL. There too. Also in Upper Michigan.

A short pause.

JANUSZ. Is that where he killed himself?

MICHAEL. No, no, that's Idaho.

Beat.

That's also very pretty.

Beat. JANUSZ *laughs to himself.*

What?

JANUSZ. Nothing.

A short pause.

MICHAEL (*while eating*). Annie and I have been thinking of spending a summer there. Right?

ANNIE. First we have to figure out how to afford it.

MICHAEL. Mostly it's the air fare.

A short pause.

My parents would love it if we came.

Beat.

They came over here about two years ago. Two years ago?

ANNIE. Yeh.

Beat.

I liked them both. Very nice people.

A short pause.

MICHAEL. They had the time of their lives, let me tell you.

Beat.

They fell for Annie in a second. And she was nervous as anything.

ANNIE. Who was nervous?

MICHAEL. What about at the airport . . .?

ANNIE. OK, OK.

Sound begins to fade out.

MICHAEL. Janusz . . .

JANUSZ. Yes?

MICHAEL. While we were waiting for my parents to clear customs, it was like Annie's jaw was frozen solid.

ANNIE. Janusz . . .

JANUSZ. Yes?

ANNIE. That was not nerves. That was a typically English expression.

ANNIE *and* MICHAEL *laugh.*

MICHAEL. They loved London, didn't they?

ANNIE. Janusz . . .

JANUSZ. Yes?

ANNIE. They loved everything about it.

MICHAEL. We started off with Buckingham Palace of course.

ANNIE. Janusz . . .

JANUSZ. Yes?

ANNIE. You're not going to believe this . . .

MICHAEL. Let me tell him. Annie had never even seen the changing
of the . . .

Sound out.

6 Janusz thanks Michael

Interior. JANUSZ*'s flat. Day.*
    JANUSZ *clears his throat. A short pause.* JANUSZ *goes to the sink, turns
on the tap and fills the kettle with water.*
    Pause.

JANUSZ. Michael?

Beat.

Have you finished reading?

Beat.

Is something the matter?

A short pause.

It stopped raining outside. Perhaps you'd like to get some air.

Beat.

You see how little I changed of what you'd done, Michael.
One word.

Beat.

Maybe two words.

Beat.

For the style only.

Pause.

MICHAEL. It's totally different.

Pause.

JANUSZ. A few words. I very much liked some of what you
had done.

MICHAEL. Janusz, you changed everything. There's hardly a line of
mine left in the ten pages.

JANUSZ. The first pages are always the most difficult. It is with
them that one learns the feeling. You are learning now the
feeling, Michael.

MICHAEL. Yeh.

Beat.

I guess.

JANUSZ. And you shall get that feeling in no time at all.

Beat.

It's all that German you've been translating. This is what confuses one. (*He laughs.*) Still some of your word choices . . . excellent.

Beat.

Excellent.

A short pause.

What do you say, today I shall join you in a cup of tea.

JANUSZ *goes to the sink. He washes a cup.*

MICHAEL. By the way, you spelled a couple of words wrong.

JANUSZ. Spelling in English! This is my nightmare! Thank you for pointing this out.

A short pause.

MICHAEL. Least there's something I can do.

JANUSZ. Michael.

Beat.

The chairs fit nicely into here, yes?

Beat.

And the lamp too. Thank you. I can't thank you and Annie enough. What a lucky man you are, Michael, with such a cook for a wife!

A short pause.

And this Michigan. What a place it must be. I can only imagine it like a dream. But perhaps I shall get the chance to visit it myself one day.

Beat.

Perhaps.

A short pause.

To bring me into your home like that. I am very grateful . . .

MICHAEL. Janusz, you don't have to try to make me feel better . . .

Beat.

I just had a different take on the book, that's all.

Beat.

Now that I see what you want . . .

JANUSZ. Of course.

Pause.

MICHAEL. I missed . . . I didn't realise you meant it to be so . . . ironic, I guess.

JANUSZ. Ironic! This is Polish literature! (*He laughs.*)

Pause.

Let me tell you a story, Michael. About Polish literature.

MICHAEL. Janusz . . .

JANUSZ. Please. I think this will help us to understand each other.

MICHAEL. I know what you're going to . . .

JANUSZ. Michael.

A short pause.

This was what? Maybe three years ago. In Warsaw of course. At our Writers' Union offices, there was a party.

Beat.

A meeting. A small meeting with music, wine and vodka.

Beat.

A party. (*He laughs to himself.*) Very small. Maybe twelve, fifteen of us all talking, meeting, putting, as one says, names to faces. I was in one corner talking to a very attractive poetess.

Beat.

I have since read her poetry and her most distinguished attribute remains her attractiveness.

The kettle boils.

One moment.

He takes the kettle off.

She knew my books of course.

MICHAEL. Of course.

As JANUSZ *continues to pour the hot water for the tea.*

JANUSZ. Occasionally at these 'meetings' someone will read a work . . . always a short work, this we make the rule; the shorter the better.

Beat.

It is maybe five o'clock in the afternoon, no one has begun to read yet, though my poetess has moved very close to me; she has her shoes off and leans against the grey wall, her arm out; and if I were to lean back as well, this arm would be around me or at least against my shoulders.

Beat.

She has lovely feet I see. She wears nylons.

Beat.

And her breath is quite warm as she asks about the women in my books. What women are you most interested in, I ask.

Beat.

The matrons or the . . . But I never got the question out, Michael, because just then the door to the hall opens and two policemen and a man who we soon hear is Russian hurry in. Someone asks what they are doing as this is a private meeting.

Beat.

The Russian . . . who is drunk, by the way . . . he turns to a small woman . . . the name doesn't matter, and with the back of his hand hits her in the face. She screams. Her nose starts to bleed. She is one of our best literary critics, this woman, an expert on Conrad. At least fifty years old as well.

Beat.

The Russian tells her to sit on the floor. He then lifts up her dress, and with a violent gesture he rips off her pants.
Her underpants.

A short pause.

I forgot to buy biscuits. I'm sorry.

MICHAEL. That's OK.

JANUSZ. Standing next to the attractive poetess, I wonder if he is going to make us all strip, when suddenly he comes right up to me and says . . .

Beat.

. . . 'The novelist Vukovski?' He'd recognised my face from a picture on one of my novels. Two have been published in Russian.

Beat.

Very popular.

Beat.

He speaks to me in Russian. He says what is he to do? He's got this old critic naked on the floor, but already he's lost his taste for her. He wonders if I would trade him my poetess for the critic.

Beat.

The critic is very important, this I know. And the poetess . . . I did not know her work. Fortunately, it turned out not to be so good as I have said, but then I did not know this. Still I took the chance. And made the trade. And with the help of the policemen, she is taken out of the room.

Beat.

You see the responsibilities thrust upon the writer in my country?

Pause.

MICHAEL. Yes.

A short pause.

Janusz . . .

JANUSZ. One moment. Now I tell you this story to make a point.

MICHAEL. Janusz, I understand the point. Because someone like me hasn't experienced this what? Hell? Suffering? Degradation? Then I can't, I don't . . . It is maybe impossible for me to ever really translate . . .

JANUSZ. Michael.

Beat.

Oh Michael.

He laughs.

MICHAEL. What?

JANUSZ. That is not my point.

Beat.

My point is . . . that you believe the story, yes?

MICHAEL. I . . .

JANUSZ. This story I just make up right now, you believed it. Not even a good story.

Beat.

Russians stay a million miles away from people like me in Poland.

Beat.

But you believe. And Michael this is your first nature, to believe what you hear, what you are told.

A short pause.

To translate Polish one must relearn one's first nature, Michael.

Beat.

One must learn to think like I do.

Beat.

One must learn that what is in front of one, what one sees and hears with one's own eyes and ears is usually what is not true.

Beat.

And certainly not to be believed.

Beat.

More tea?

Fade out.

7 Janusz gives a dinner and a shawl

Interior (later exterior). JANUSZ'*s flat. Evening.* MICHAEL, ANNIE, JANUSZ *and* JAN KOSTKA *having dinner.*

MICHAEL. Delicious curry.

ANNIE. Yes. You must have quite a good Indian place in the area.

JANUSZ. Yes. Yes, there is.

Beat.

Very nice.

A short pause.

JAN (*in Czech*). What did they say?

JANUSZ (*in Czech*). They like the food.

JAN (*in Czech*). It's from the corner?

JANUSZ (*in Czech*). The place on Edgware Road is much cheaper.

Pause. They eat.

MICHAEL. Yes. Very nice.

JAN (*in Czech*). What?

JANUSZ (to JAN, *in Czech*). Why don't you try to speak Polish? He understands Polish. (*To* MICHAEL, *in English:*) I am trying to convince Jan to try to speak Polish.

MICHAEL. Oh. He speaks . . .

JANUSZ. Not too good. But . . .

MICHAEL. I'm sorry I don't speak Czech.

ANNIE. Does he know any German? Michael's fluent in German, and I can sort of follow along . . .

JANUSZ. No.

Beat.

He doesn't speak German.

Beat.

(*In Czech:*) You don't speak German do you?

JAN (*in Czech*). *No*.

JANUSZ. He said . . .

MICHAEL. Yes. We figured that out.

A short pause. They eat.

How long has Jan been here, Janusz?

JANUSZ. He arrived only before you and Annie did.

MICHAEL. No. I meant . . .

JANUSZ. Oh, in England you mean. Four months.

Beat.

That was stupid of me when you asked . . .

MICHAEL. Not at all. I wasn't being clear.

A short pause.

JANUSZ. Four months he's been here. (*In Czech:*) *You've been here four months, right?*

JAN (*in Czech*). *It's been more than four months, Janusz. It is May, yes? I came in December. So that's December, January, February, March, April and May. That's six months.*

Beat.

Almost six months.

Beat.

JANUSZ (*in English*). Don't pay any attention to him. He's been here four months.

MICHAEL. Ah.

Pause. They eat.

JANUSZ. Michael, perhaps you could tell Jan where the Czechs are in America.

MICHAEL. Where the Czechs are?

Beat.

I'm sorry, I don't understand.

JANUSZ. Like the Poles are in this Michigan. Where are the Czechs?

A short pause.

MICHAEL. Probably all around the country.

Beat.

I don't know to be honest.

JANUSZ (*in Czech*). *He doesn't know where the Czechs are in America.*

JAN (*in Czech*). *There are no Czechs in America.*

JANUSZ (*in Czech*). *That can't be true.*
(*In English:*) Jan says there are no Czechs in America.

ANNIE. I doubt if that's . . .

JAN (*in Czech*). *Once you go to America you become American.*

JANUSZ. Ah.

Beat.

He says you go to America you become American. Not
Czech anymore.

MICHAEL. Oh (*He laughs.*) Yes. I guess in a way that's true. That's
sort of what worries Annie actually.

ANNIE. What worries me?

MICHAEL. I think that's why you're a little hesitant about going to
the States. Even for a short visit.

Beat.

Let alone moving there.

JANUSZ. You're thinking of moving . . .?

ANNIE. No.

Beat.

No, we're not, Janusz.

A short pause.

MICHAEL. She's afraid, Janusz of losing something of herself.

ANNIE. I never said that, Michael.

MICHAEL. Not in those words . . .

ANNIE. Then that means I never said it.

Beat.

What would *I* do in the States?

MICHAEL. That's why I've been suggesting we just go for a short . . .

JANUSZ. One moment, please. Stop, please. Let me translate.
(*In Czech:*) *They're talking about moving or just visiting the States. Michael
says she is afraid of losing something of herself. She says she doesn't know
what she will do there.*

JAN (*in Czech*). *I understand.*

JANUSZ. You can continue now.

A short pause.

ANNIE. I'm not worried about visiting your parents in the States.

MICHAEL. I know you're not.

Beat.

Janusz, could I get some more wine?

JANUSZ. Of course. Here, let me. I'm sorry.

Pause.

ANNIE. Janusz, have you thought any more about my father's cottage?

JAN (*in Czech*). *What's this?*

JANUSZ (*in Czech*). *They have offered me the use of a cottage in the country.*

JAN (*in Czech*). *Where is it?*

JANUSZ. Where was it again?

ANNIE. East Sussex.

Beat.

Not terribly far really.

JAN. East Sussex?

ANNIE. Yes.

JAN (*in Czech*). *Are you going to use it?*

JANUSZ (*in Czech*). *I doubt it. Why would I want to go to the . . .*

JAN (*in Czech*). *Then I'll use it.*

JANUSZ (*in Czech*). *Jan, they asked me.*

JAN (*in Czech*). *If it's just sitting there . . .*

JANUSZ. Excuse us. (*In Czech:*) *I can't just . . .*

JAN (*in Czech*). *Why not, if they're offering. Ask them.*

Beat.

Ask them.

A short pause.

JANUSZ. Jan says if I don't use the cottage he would like to.

Beat.

But I told him . . .

ANNIE. No. No.

Beat.

I'll have to ask my father, of course. But I'm sure, he'll . . .

Beat.

Make sure we get his number before we go.

JAN (*in Czech*). *Tell them I used to have a cottage about fifty-five kilometres outside of Prague.*

JANUSZ. Jan says he used to have a cottage outside of Prague.

JAN (*in Czech*). *And if they are ever in Prague, I know the woman who has it now.*

JANUSZ. And if you are ever in Prague, the woman who has the cottage now, he knows.

MICHAEL. Oh.

Beat.

Thank you.

ANNIE. Thank you, Jan.

Pause. JANUSZ *gets up out of his seat.*

JANUSZ. Excuse me.

He walks to a closet, opens the door, takes something out and walks back to the table.

Here.

ANNIE. What's . . .?

JANUSZ. It is for you. Actually it is to thank both of you. But I thought . . .

Beat.

Open it.

MICHAEL. Open it, Annie.

ANNIE. Janusz, I hope you didn't spend your money on . . .

She has opened the package.

It's beautiful. Look Michael.

MICHAEL. What is it?

ANNIE. A shawl?

JANUSZ. Yes.

Beat.

I found it in a stall at Covent Garden.

Beat.

I think it's Polish.

JAN (*in Czech*). *Let me see.*

JANUSZ. He wants to see.

Beat.

It's for the chairs. And the lamp.

(*In Czech:*) *They loaned me these chairs.*

JAN (*in Czech*). *Nice chairs. Have they any more to loan?*

JANUSZ (*in Czech*). *Jan, I can't ask* –

JAN (*in Czech*). *Ask. Why not?*

ANNIE. What? Does Jan want something?

JANUSZ. He wants to know if you have any more chairs.

MICHAEL. Any more chairs?

JANUSZ. I told him you loaned . . .

MICHAEL. Oh.

> *Beat.*

> Well, I'm sure we probably do. We must make sure to get Jan's number, Annie.

JANUSZ (*in Czech*). *They have more chairs.*

JAN (*in Czech*). *I told you, Janusz.*

> *Pause.*

ANNIE. The shawl's hand embroidered, isn't it?

JANUSZ. Yes.

> *A short pause.*

ANNIE. Janusz, you really shouldn't be spending your money on us.

> *Beat.*

> On me.

JANUSZ. It is the least I can do to pay you both back.

MICHAEL. Janusz, but we've told you, taking those chairs was actually doing us a . . .

JAN (*in Czech*). *You gave the shawl to her?*

JANUSZ (*in Czech*). *Yes.*

JAN (*in Czech*). *And not to your wife, Marie? She would love such a shawl.*

JANUSZ (*shouts, in Czech*). *I didn't buy it for Marie!*

MICHAEL. What? What did he say?

JAN (*in Czech*). *She's there with your children* . . .

JANUSZ (*in Czech*). *I gave it to* . . .

ANNIE. Who's Marie?

JANUSZ. My wife.

MICHAEL. He knows your wife?

JANUSZ. We've known each other for many years. He's a good friend of my wife's.

JAN (*in Czech*). *A shawl like this would have made her so happy.*

MICHAEL. What's he saying?

JANUSZ. Nothing.

JAN (*in Czech*). *Right now, she is wondering if you even remember her.*

JANUSZ. He says I should have given the shawl to my wife.

ANNIE. Yes. Of course he's right. Here.

JANUSZ. But I didn't buy it for my wife. I bought it for you, who have been so kind to me.

ANNIE. Really, it would make me feel . . .

JANUSZ (*yells*). No!!!

> *Pause.*

JAN (*in Czech*). *You ought to be ashamed of yourself.*

ANNIE. What did he say?

JANUSZ. That I should be ashamed.

JAN (*in Czech*). *And it would serve you right if Marie were in bed with someone right this minute.*

JANUSZ. And that it would serve me right if my wife were in bed with someone this very minute.

> *Pause. An awkward silence.*

MICHAEL. More wine anyone?

ANNIE. I would, please, Michael.

MICHAEL. Janusz?

JANUSZ. No.

> *A short pause.*

MICHAEL. Jan?

JAN (*in Czech*). *I never say no to French wine.*

JANUSZ. He says he can't say no to French wine.

MICHAEL. It's Italian wine.

JAN (*in Czech*). *Or Italian wine.*

JANUSZ. Or Italian wine.

> *Fade out and cut to: Exterior. The street. Night.* MICHAEL *and* ANNIE *walking to the tube.*
> *Pause.*

ANNIE. That was nice.

> *A short pause.*

That was interesting.

MICHAEL. Are you really going to talk to your father . . .?

ANNIE. About Jan using the cottage? Of course not. You saw how much he smoked.

Beat.

Even during dinner.

Beat.

I didn't know people did that anymore. While other people are eating.

Beat.

I'm afraid he'd burn the cottage down.

A short pause.

MICHAEL. I forgot to get his number.

ANNIE. Oh well.

Pause as they walk.

MICHAEL. Beautiful shawl.

ANNIE. I wish he hadn't spent . . . And Jan was right, he should have sent it to his wife. Think of what it must be like for her.

MICHAEL. But I guess he felt he owed us so much . . .

ANNIE. That's silly.

MICHAEL. I know that.

Beat.

You know that.

Beat.

But . . .

A short pause.

It was obviously just very important for him not to feel too . . . I don't know, in debt, I guess, to someone else.

Beat.

For his own self-respect, I mean.

Beat.

So this was his way of paying us back.

ANNIE. The curry was awful.

MICHAEL. Wasn't it?

Beat.

ANNIE. So anyway, in his mind, we're all even now.

MICHAEL. Yes.

Beat.

Now we're even.

Fade out.

8 Michael thanks Janusz

Interior. JANUSZ's flat. Day.
 Sound effect: door buzzer. Pause. Buzzer. A short pause. Buzzer. Footsteps.
JANUSZ *opens the door.*

JANUSZ. Sorry, I'm just on the telephone. (*As they walk back in:*)
   Michael, you know where the kettle is.

MICHAEL. Don't worry about me. Take your time.

A short pause.

JANUSZ (*into the phone*). Hello, yes. That sounds good, yes.

Beat.

No, I don't. But I take your word for it.

Beat.

Uh-huh. But could we talk about this later. Michael Milick has
just come in.

Beat.

Yes. Thank you. Goodbye.

He hangs up. A short pause.

You didn't put the kettle on.

JANUSZ *turns on the tap and fills the kettle. Pause.*

Sit down, please Michael.

Beat.

I apologise, I haven't had time to get your biscuits for
this morning.

Beat.

But I could go right . . .

MICHAEL. Janusz, I don't need any biscuits.

JANUSZ. No?

MICHAEL. No. Really.

Beat.

Who was on the phone?

JANUSZ. You mean now? Come on, sit down, you shouldn't wait to be asked, Michael.

A short pause.

I hope my friend, Jan, didn't . . . how do you say it? Put you off last night.

MICHAEL. Not at all. Annie and I adored him.

JANUSZ. Good. He liked both of you very much.

MICHAEL. I'm glad.

JANUSZ. He's a very witty man . . . in Czech.

MICHAEL. I gathered this.

A short pause.

It was a wonderful evening.

Beat.

JANUSZ. Let me get your cup. Today I think I shall join with you and have some tea.

He goes to sink and washes cups.

MICHAEL. I'm sorry if I'm a little early, Janusz.

JANUSZ. You're early?

Beat.

I did not realise.

A short pause.

MICHAEL. There's nothing the matter, is there, Janusz?

JANUSZ. No, what could be the matter?

Pause.

MICHAEL. Have you had the chance to go over the last twenty pages I gave you?

JANUSZ. Yes, yes, of course. Here. Look here. Hardly a single change or suggestion.

MICHAEL (*after a short pause*). I'm amazed.

Beat.

Grateful, but still amazed.

JANUSZ. It's the feeling. I told you once one gets the feeling then . . .

MICHAEL. Then I've finally gotten what you want.

Beat.

This is what you want.

Beat.

You are happy with this? Is that right? I don't want you to . . . Just because . . .

JANUSZ. Just because what?

MICHAEL. Because we're . . . well, friends.

JANUSZ. No, no, I wouldn't do that.

MICHAEL. Good.

A short pause.

I have to admit I've started feeling a lot better about my work. I do think I've started to hear your voice . . .

JANUSZ. Yes, yes.

A short pause.

MICHAEL. Well, let's hope it's not a fluke and the next ten pages are as good.

JANUSZ. I'm sure . . .

MICHAEL. Well, let's see, right?

Beat.

Just keep being tough on me, OK?

JANUSZ. OK.

A short pause.

MICHAEL. Nothing's wrong? You haven't heard something about your wife and children?

JANUSZ. No, no.

Beat.

What could be wrong?

MICHAEL. I don't know, you seem . . .

JANUSZ. That's the wine from last night, not wanting to leave my head. (*He laughs.* MICHAEL *laughs.*)

MICHAEL. Yes, that could be it.

A short pause.

JANUSZ (*suddenly energetic*). Oh, you asked who was on the phone.

MICHAEL. Only because I heard you mention my name . . . as if they knew me.

JANUSZ. Yes, of course he knows you. You introduced us, in a way.

Beat.

John Robertson at Fabers.

MICHAEL. John? I didn't know you two . . .

The kettle boils.

JANUSZ. Excuse me.

The kettle stops boiling.

Didn't I tell you? We had lunch together just the other day.

Beat.

I thought I told you, Michael.

MICHAEL. No, you didn't.

Beat.

What did he want? Did you give him some chapters?

JANUSZ. Yes and he's reading them. That's what he called to say.

MICHAEL. He called to say he was reading them?

JANUSZ. Yes.

MICHAEL. Just to say that?

JANUSZ. Yes.

MICHAEL. Not that he liked what he'd read, only that he was still . . .?

JANUSZ. Yes.

Beat.

Here's your tea.

Pause.

He took me to a restaurant in Chelsea.

Beat.

We ate Italian.

Pause.

Faber & Faber, this is T.S. Eliot's publisher, yes?

MICHAEL. It was. It is.

Beat.

He worked there too. And they published his books.

A short pause.

JANUSZ. Eliot is a very good poet, Michael. One of your best. I like Eliot.

MICHAEL. Good.

A short pause.

JANUSZ. And Ezra Pound, no?

MICHAEL. They also publish Pound.

JANUSZ. Very overrated poet, I think. In Polish his poems read like drivel.

MICHAEL. Maybe it's the translations.

JANUSZ. Yes? I guess that could be.

A short pause.

But Eliot . . . Very important.

Beat.

This would be a good place for my book?

MICHAEL. Yes. Definitely.

Beat.

If they show any interest at all, we should kill to get it published there.

JANUSZ. Yes.

Fade out.

9 Janusz plays his cards

Interior. MICHAEL *and* ANNIE's *flat:* MICHAEL's *study. Afternoon.* MICHAEL *typing. Pause. A knock on the door. After a moment the door opens.* MICHAEL *continues to type.*

MICHAEL. What are you doing home?

Beat.

Just a second.

He types, then stops.

What time is it?

ANNIE. Half past two.

Beat.

Carol thought I should come home.

MICHAEL. Is anything wrong? Are you sick?

ANNIE. No.

Beat.

No, I'm not sick.

Beat.

Carol thought it'd be best if I were the one to tell you.

Beat.

She said she'd do it of course, but . . .

MICHAEL. You were the one to tell me what, Annie?

ANNIE. Carol's really upset. You know, you are more than just a client to her.

MICHAEL. Annie! Please what are you talking about?

ANNIE. Actually it's unbelievable. I don't understand really.

Beat.

John Robertson . . .

MICHAEL. Of Fabers. Yes.

ANNIE. He called Carol today. He said he suddenly remembered a conversation he'd had with you about . . . oh six weeks ago.

MICHAEL. I called him about Janusz's book. And Janusz told me this morning . . .

ANNIE. Wait.

Beat.

He said, well, he wanted you . . . through Carol of course . . . to know that Mr Vukovski had been to see him.

MICHAEL. I know this. They had lunch.

ANNIE. Been to see him with someone else's tranlsation of his book.

A short pause.

MICHAEL. Say that again.

ANNIE. It seems Janusz has been working with someone else on translating his book, Michael.

Beat.

They've been working for over a month now.

MICHAEL. Annie, I can't believe . . .

ANNIE. It's true. Carol called Janusz and he confessed it.

A short pause.

Hey, he's a son of a bitch, what can you do?

A short pause.

He gets you to do the legwork, you make the connections . . . Carol's never going to deal with Janusz again, I can tell you that.

Beat.

Michael, I'm sorry.

MICHAEL. Who's the other translator?

ANNIE. Some Polish friend of his, I think.

MICHAEL. For Christ's sake, why didn't he just . . . I would have just stopped.

Beat.

And Fabers?

ANNIE. They like the book.

Beat.

Though Carol thinks if we kicked up a fuss, they'd shelve it.

MICHAEL. Shelve it?

ANNIE. It's already been bought.

Beat.

The other translator has already been paid an advance.

Beat.

And this you won't believe. Robertson says Janusz wants to use a few things from your work, sort of incorporate them in the other translation.

Beat.

We think that Janusz would have been only too happy to take what he wanted without even asking. But Robertson is putting a stop to that.

Beat.

This isn't Poland after all.

Beat.

They'll need your permission.

Pause.

MICHAEL. Hell. (*He laughs to himself.*) Look what I've been writing: a letter to *The Times*. I was going to send it around and get some big signatures on it, I'd hoped.

Beat.

It's a plea for the release of Janusz's wife and all three kids.

A short pause.

ANNIE. To hell with that.

A short pause.

Michael, I really am . . . I'll get Carol, she wanted to speak to you as soon as . . . I don't understand, he said nothing last night at dinner.

MICHAEL. Or this morning.

> *Beat.*

I saw him just this morning. He didn't say a thing to me.

ANNIE *dials the phone.*

MICHAEL (*into the phone*). Hello, Carol? Michael.

> *Beat.*

Yeah, what can you do with someone like that . . . what the hell can you do?

> *Fade out.*

10 Janusz is granted another favour

Interior. JANUSZ's *flat. Afternoon.*
   The door buzzer. JANUSZ's *footsteps as he goes to the door. He opens the door.*

JANUSZ. Annie, what a nice surprise.

> *Beat.*

Come in, come in.

> *They come into the flat.*

Sit down.

ANNIE. I brought Michael's signed permission.

> *Beat.*

So you can use his . . .

JANUSZ. Thank you.

> *Beat.*

But you needn't have come. The post would have been soon enough.

> *Beat.*

But I appreciate this. It must not have been an easy thing to give. This permission.

ANNIE. Janusz . . .

JANUSZ. Say what you want to say, Annie.

ANNIE. Janusz, people don't behave the way you did in civilised countries.

JANUSZ. Poland is civilised too. For many years now.

Beat.

Keep Poland out of this, yes?

A short pause.

Is he outside?

ANNIE. No.

JANUSZ. I would have thanked him in person.

A short pause.

Annie, let me be very blunt.

ANNIE. Please. Be blunt. Or at the very least be honest for
a change.

JANUSZ. Michael's work was not very good. His Polish is not . . .

ANNIE. So then why didn't you just tell him? Instead you work with
him for a month.

JANUSZ. I wanted to. I tried to.

Beat.

I thought maybe I could help him.

Beat.

And I did for some time. But . . .

A short pause.

ANNIE. He went out and found you a publisher.

JANUSZ. He helped in this, yes.

Beat.

And so my actions do not look so good, I admit.

Beat.

But it is not like the book was never heard of.

ANNIE. Actually it is exactly like that.

JANUSZ. In Warsaw it is very successful.

A short pause.

I am very grateful for what Michael did. Please, sit down. They are
your chairs.

ANNIE. He considered you a friend.

JANUSZ. I am his . . .

ANNIE. And then you made him feel like a fool!

JANUSZ. Michael is no fool. I am sure translating German, he is
much more . . .

ANNIE. I didn't mean as a translator, Janusz.

Beat.

Jesus Christ, he was doing you a favour and you turn around and . . .

JANUSZ. I am very sorry how it must look. After all, I have to live here, yes? I don't want to be thought of in a bad way.

Beat.

But to answer you, first *I* did not consider that he was doing me a favour.

ANNIE. He didn't even like the damn book.

JANUSZ. No.

Beat.

No, that is not true.

ANNIE. He thought it was stupid.

JANUSZ. No.

Beat.

Maybe.

Beat.

Annie, I always made it very clear that I was first interested in making the book as good as it could be in English. I never hid this. And this is all I was doing.

ANNIE. To make it as successful as it could be you mean.

JANUSZ. Whatever. Whatever the criteria are. I do not know yet.

ANNIE. And this permits you to take advantage . . .

JANUSZ. Perhaps!

Beat.

All I do know is that being nice and doing favours has nothing to do with writing books or making art.

Beat.

Being nice and doing favours is what one does between writing books and making art. While one is waiting to write the book or while resting from making the art. Friends are needed then.

A short pause.

And Michael has been a very good friend. And I think I have been a very good friend to Michael.

ANNIE. Right. (*She laughs to herself.*)

JANUSZ (*almost yelling now*). Annie, if it was friendships I was most after . . . MY FRIENDS ARE IN WARSAW!!

Beat.

If I did not write books, I could have stayed with my friends in Warsaw.

Beat.

Is not this obvious about me?!

Beat.

I can think of nothing more obvious about me than this.

A short pause.

You think I came to England to be your friend?

Beat.

This is not to say I do not wish to be your friend, Annie, or that I shall not try to be a good friend to you. But for God's sake, please be fair to me!!!

Pause.

I am sorry if Michael is hurt. He will get over it very soon.

Beat.

A bad translation, my book will never get over.

ANNIE. OK.

Beat.

I guess we pushed ourselves too much on you.

JANUSZ. That is not what I am saying!

A short pause.

ANNIE. I was brought up to take my time getting to know someone, just to prevent this sort of . . .

JANUSZ. Annie, damnit, you are not listening to me!!

ANNIE. We had you over to dinner.

JANUSZ. I had you too.

A short pause.

Let me put the tea on.

ANNIE. We gave you chairs.

JANUSZ. Loaned them to me.

Beat.

I gave you that shawl.

ANNIE. Which I brought back. I don't want it anymore.

JANUSZ. Annie, no.

Beat.

No.

ANNIE. Give it to your wife.

JANUSZ. No.

Pause.

ANNIE. We went so far out of our way to help you.

JANUSZ. I know.

Beat.

Thank you.

Pause as he turns the tap on and fills the kettle.

ANNIE (*finally*). Is this how you treated your friends back in Warsaw?!

JANUSZ. Annie, I did much worse to them.

Beat.

I came here.

Fade out.

11 Michael plays his cards

Interior. Restaurant (Chelsea). Lunchtime.

WAITER. More coffee, gentlemen?

ANDREW. None for me. Two cups is my limit.

MICHAEL. No, thank you.

A short pause.

ANDREW. Michael, would you like a taste of my pie?

MICHAEL. No thanks.

ANDREW. I've never eaten here.

MICHAEL. It's only something like three months old.

A short pause.

ANDREW. So anyway, you in the end gave Vukosovic your permission.

MICHAEL. Yes. What could I do?

Beat.

How would it have looked?

Beat.

He has no money. He hardly knows anyone.

ANDREW. He knew another translator.

MICHAEL. I'm not bitter, Andrew.

ANDREW. I can't say I'd blame you if you were. If I were in your shoes . . .

MICHAEL. You'd be acting the same way.

Beat.

Once I got over the initial shock . . . the sense of betrayal . . . I soon realised there was little *I* could do.

A short pause.

ANDREW. Anyone going to review this book?

MICHAEL. I had lunch last week with Lester . . .

ANDREW. He's still at the *Review of Books*?

MICHAEL. Yes.

Beat.

He isn't going to touch it. No review. Nothing.

Beat.

That's a shame, I think.

Beat.

It's not a bad book, really. A little obscure for a British . . . and certainly for an American . . . audience. But . . . . Worthy of some sort of review.

ANDREW (*eating his pie*). Well . . . serves him right, if you ask me. This sort of behaviour, I'd hate to see it encouraged. What about the dailies?

MICHAEL. Lester doubted if there'd be anything.

Beat.

He was going to talk to some people.

Beat.

He was very put off by the way I was treated. I couldn't convince him that I didn't care . . .

ANDREW. Lester would be put off. He's a man of high moral standards.

MICHAEL. As you are, Andrew.

ANDREW. I like to think so, yes.

Pause.

MICHAEL. In the end, what I feel most for Janusz is pity. And to think he brought it all on himself.

Beat.

Really, didn't he know that no one would want to work with someone who acted like . . .

ANDREW. Yes, it's not like he were bloody Samuel Beckett or something, then . . . well. But he's not, of course.

Beat.

This play he gave me, well, it's OK. It's just OK.

MICHAEL. I felt the same way when I read it in Polish.

ANDREW. I have to confess I was leaning a little toward doing it. It is after all . . . OK.

Beat.

And how many plays are OK today? (*He laughs to himself.*)

MICHAEL. Janusz will be terribly excited to hear this.

ANDREW. But to be honest I'm beginning to change my mind.

MICHAEL. I hope not because of . . .

ANDREW. You do a man's play, well, you spend a lot of time with the man. And life is only so long, Michael.

Beat.

I may just send the script right back.

MICHAEL. But if it's worth doing . . .

ANDREW. It's only OK, Michael. Nothing more.

Pause.

MICHAEL. He really has screwed things up for himself, hasn't he?

ANDREW. Indeed so, Michael. Indeed.

WAITER. Anything else, gentlemen?

MICHAEL. Just the check.

Beat.

Andrew, please, this is on me. I really do insist.

ANDREW. Then, thank you, Michael. Thank you very much.

MICHAEL. You're welcome.

Fade out.

THE VILLAGE FÊTE

by Peter Tinniswood

For the producer of *Village Fête*, Shaun MacLoughlin, and the actors, Maurice Denham, Shirley Dixon, Christian Rodska, Liz Goulding, Carole Boyd and, of course, Bill Wallis.

Peter Tinniswood, playwright, novelist and broadcaster, was born in Liverpool. He has written fourteen books and novels. His most famous creations are Uncle Mort and the Brigadier, both of whom have also appeared on radio, television and the stage. Among his stage plays are two written for and directed by Alan Ayckbourn, *You Should See Us Now* having been performed at Greenwich. He has written a few plays for television and numerous plays for radio, which is his favourite medium. He is currently working on a new stage play for Alan Ayckbourn and a drama-documentary series for BBC Television.

The Village Fête was first broadcast on BBC Radio 4 on 17 January 1987. The cast was as follows:

NANCY   Shirley Dixon
FATHER   Maurice Denham
ROSIE   Liz Goulding
WINSTON   Bill Wallis
WILLIAM   Christian Rodska
MRS GODWIN   Carole Boyd
STANLEY   Ronald Herdman
JANET   Jennifer Piercey

Director: Shaun MacLoughlin
Running time, as broadcast: 87 minutes, 25 seconds

1

NANCY (*to mike*). We moved from London to the country on a
misty morning in early May.
There were no blackheaded gulls.
Thrushes sang.
Next door neighbour's cat howled.
And the house spider came out from his hole by the fireplace in
the drawing-room to bid us goodbye.
He seemed so smug about it all.
The removal men couldn't park outside the house.
But, of course.
William got distraught.
But, of course.

WILLIAM. It's so outrageously inconvenient.

ROSIE. Moving house is always inconvenient, William.

WILLIAM. But it's specifically inconvenient to me, Rosie.
I am approaching the climax of my book.
It's all locked away in my head.
I am rapidly reaching the denouement.
Do you understand?
The denouement.
And this move will absolutely destroy it.

ROSIE. How can anyone possibly have a denouement in a book
about the Dorset and Somerset Railway?

WILLIAM. It is not the Dorset and Somerset Railway. It is the
Somerset and Dorset Railways, if you must know.

ROSIE. Oh, I'm so sorry, William.
That makes all the difference, doesn't it?

WILLIAM. Oh, mockery, mockery.
You can sneer.
But if it weren't for these books of mine which you dismiss so
contemptuously, a major part of the income of this household
would be lost forever.
And then where would we be?

ROSIE. Ah yes.
The old story.
Now let me see.
It was the Great Central Railway which paid for the re-wiring.
It was the Cambrian Coast Line which bought us the new
bathroom suite in avocado.
It was the . . .

WILLIAM. My God, why did I ever stick with this family? I could
have lived on my own and enjoyed a degree of fame and esteem I
never remotely touch in this bloody household.

ROSIE. You get esteem, William.
You get esteem.
You drag it out of us, screaming and kicking.
You are the most thoroughly spoiled man I ever met in the whole
of my life.

WILLIAM. Me?
Spoiled?

ROSIE. Yes.

WILLIAM. Well, if being spoiled is allowing myself to be dragged
away from my roots where I'm happy to live in the godforsaken
countryside, then you've got a very funny idea of the meaning of
the word.

ROSIE. There's no need for you to come.
Stay.

WILLIAM. You know perfectly well I can't stay.

ROSIE. Why?

WILLIAM. Well . . . well, you know why.

ROSIE. No, I don't, William.
You're a very self-contained man.
A loner.
You prefer your own company.
That's what you're always telling us.
So stay and fend for yourself.
I'd have thought you'd manage very well.
A nice little bed-sitter in Belsize Park, maybe.
You know – tatty velvet curtains and a threadbare Indian carpet
and one of those gas rings hidden away in a fitted wardrobe.

And a landlady who slip-slops round the house with a cigarette
permanently stuck to her lower lip.
And cat hairs and the smell of cabbage and the . . .
You'd love it, William.

WILLIAM. You know perfectly well it would kill me.

ROSIE. That's why you've got to move with us then, isn't it,
William?

WILLIAM. Father's chest.
Why have we always got to move because of Father?
Father's chest, Father's legs, Father's headaches, Father's . . .

ROSIE. We move because we love Father.

WILLIAM. Oh do we?

ROSIE. Yes, we do.

WILLIAM. Well, I don't.
At this moment I do not love Father.

ROSIE. Yes, you do.

WILLIAM. No, I don't.

ROSIE. You do, you do . . .

Fade on argument.

2

NANCY (*to mike*). We are what is called a talented family.
My brother, William, is an author.
My sister, Rosie, is a designer of textiles.
My father before his retirement was the headmaster of a most
prestigious private school.
And my talent?
My talent is in keeping us all together.

She laughs bitterly.

After the removal men had left Rosie and I scrubbed down the
house from top to bottom.
William sat on the floor in his empty study and sulked.
I called to the house spider.
But he didn't appear.
He didn't want to know us now.
We'd deserted him.
I went into the garden to look for Father.

Garden sounds.

Father, Father.

FATHER. There's a thrush singing, Nancy.

NANCY. I know.

FATHER. I like the sound of thrushes.

NANCY. You'll hear lots and lots of thrushes in the country, Father.

FATHER. I know.
But I shall miss the city thrushes.

A jumbo jet passes low overhead.

I shall miss the jumbo jets, too.

NANCY. No, you won't, Father.

FATHER. Yes, I will.
I used to like watching them passing overhead and wondering
where they were going to.
Afghanistan, maybe?
Australia, Malta, India.
The sky's the limit, eh?

NANCY. Come along, Father.
It's time to go.

FATHER. Yes.
Yes, another house to say farewell to.

NANCY. We're getting quite expert at it, aren't we, Father?

FATHER. Yes.
It's my chest, you see.
I need the fresh air of the country.

NANCY. Of course you do, Father.

FATHER. You see, when we lived by the sea it was my sinuses that
couldn't cope.
And when we lived . . .

NANCY. I know, Father, I know.
Come along.
(*To mike:*) I took him by the arm.
I led him through the garden.
And the thrush flew off.
I led him into the drawing-room and he said:

3

FATHER. Has the house spider shown himself, Nancy?

NANCY. Yes, he came out to say goodbye.
He's gone now.

FATHER. Yes.
  I don't blame him.

NANCY (*to mike*). We got into the car and drove off.
  We hadn't been able to park outside the house.
  But, of course.

  Interior car noise.

WILLIAM. I hate motorways.

ROSIE. You hate everything today, William.

WILLIAM. That is not true, Rosie.
  My hatred for motorways is long-established and well known in
  the family.
  I mean, look at all this traffic.
  Juggernauts, coaches, petrol tankers.
  Now if we only transferred them all to rail, we'd have a well-
  organised, well-integrated rationalised transport system.
  I've said it time and time again in my books.
  I've written umpteen articles in newspapers, magazines . . .
  Why are you pulling my sleeve, Father?

FATHER. I want to tell you something.
  I used to like travelling by rail.

ROSIE. Did you, Father?

FATHER. Yes.
  I once made a trip across India by rail.
  With your mother.

ROSIE. How exciting.

FATHER. Yes, it was.
  I can't remember a thing about it.
  Except that it was exciting.
  Yes.
  We ate a lot of curry, if my memory serves me correct.

WILLIAM. I quite like curry.

FATHER. You take after your mother.
  She liked curry.

NANCY. We all like curry, Father.

ROSIE. I don't.

WILLIAM. Well, that's news to me.
  You always used to like it.

ROSIE. I don't like it now.

WILLIAM. Rubbish.

ROSIE. I do not like curry now, and if I am challenged any more on
  the subject I shall go screaming mad.

NANCY. That's enough, Rosie
  I have to drive.
  I have to keep my eyes on the road.
  I do not wish to be distracted by my family squabbling and
  shouting.
  So calm it.
  Calm down.
  Calm down, shall we, everyone?

ROSIE (*very softly and icily*). Yes, Nancy.
  Anything you say.
  But, of course.

NANCY (*to mike*). And so we reached the village where we were
  going to live.
  I drove down the main street with its potholes and stains from
  tractor tyres.
  I drove past the pub, past the old farmstead and the shifty-eyed
  council houses and turned left up the narrow lane with its rutted
  cart tracks and its sobbing willows.
  And there was our house.
  Yes, I could really keep them in order here.

The noise of a helicopter passing low overhead.

FATHER. I say, it's got helicopters.

NANCY. Of course it has, Father.
  That's why I know you're going to like it.

FATHER. Army helicopters, too.
  Very good.
  Very good indeed.
  I'm going to like this place – provided my legs hold out, of
  course.

ROSIE (*softly and icily*). But, of course, Father.
  Of course.

NANCY (*to mike*). And so we opened the front door and stepped into
  our new house.

4

ROSIE. I can smell gas.

WILLIAM. So can I.

NANCY. Put your pipe out, Father.

FATHER. Pardon?

NANCY. Your pipe, Father.

Put it out.
There's a smell of gas.

FATHER. I can't smell a thing, Nancy.
It's my sinuses, you see.
All those years of neglect.
All those . . .

ROSIE. Ring the emergency service.

WILLIAM. What?

ROSIE. Ring the emergency service.

WILLIAM. But how will I know its number?

NANCY. Look in the phone book, William.
It'll be under . . .
Never mind, I'll do it.
And put out that pipe, Father.
You'll blow us all to smithereens.

FATHER. Mm. Yes.
There is one consolation, though.

WILLIAM. What is that, Father?

FATHER. We can park the car outside the house.

NANCY (*to mike*). The emergency men came and discovered that we
had a 22 per cent gas leak.
And it was rising.
So they cut off our gas.
And so we had no heating and we had no cooking.
And in the middle of all this while they were digging up the road
outside the house to find the mains the removal men arrived.
They could not park outside.
But of course.

WILLIAM. Mind what you're doing with that desk.
For God's sake be careful.
The drawers are still full.
All my notes are there.
Be careful.

ROSIE. And be careful with my table.
Don't kick it.
That is an antique table.
It's priceless.
Good Lord, you're ripping it to bits.

NANCY. Please. Rosie. Please, William.
Calm down.
Calm down.
Everything's going to be all right.

FATHER. I've just discovered a shed at the bottom of the garden.

NANCY. Have you really, Father?

FATHER. Yes.
It'll be absolutely perfect for smoking my pipe in.

ROSIE. Oh good.
I'm so pleased for you, Father.
We're all pleased.

FATHER. How kind of you to say so, Rosie.
How agreeable.
Well then, I think I'll potter off back there.
Have a pipe or something.
Don't want me here with these gas wallahs, do you?
Never was very good with gas.
Or with electricity, if it comes to that.
Always was absolutely useless round the house.
That's what your mother used to say.
She used to say to me:
'You're absolutely useless round the house.'
And I was.
Absolutely useless.

NANCY (*to mike*). And then the emergency men condemned
the boiler.
They said we had to have a new one.
They put a notice on the old boiler.
It said 'Condemned'.
I felt sorry for the poor little thing crouching there all forlorn like
a dog you're taking to the vets to be put down.
I wanted to cuddle it.
How long will it take to get a new one, I asked.
Oh, about three or four weeks, they said.
Charming, I said, absolutely lovely.
And Rosie ground her teeth.
And William repaired to his study and sat on a packing case
and sulked.

WILLIAM. I hate today.
I hate it, hate it, hate it.

NANCY (*to mike*). The removal men left us.
They had a look of pity on their faces.
They were going back to warm homes and street-corner shops
and clacking pavements and workmen's cafés with spitting
bacon.
They were leaving us in a wasteland of tea chests, plastic sacks
and sullen cardboard boxes.
And the place stank of gas.
And it stank of dampness.

And we looked at each other and Rosie began to cry softly and
William quivered his lower lip like he used to do when he was a
little boy and Father fell asleep and his pipe dropped from his
mouth and showered the front of his cardigan with red-hot
burning embers.
And I looked at them and I said to myself:
Poor you.
What would you do without me?
How could we survive?

Pause. Then a ring on the front door.

WILLIAM. Who's that?

ROSIE. What a stupid thing to say, William.
How can we possibly know who it is until we answer the door?
Do you think I've got X-ray eyes?
Do you think I've . . .

NANCY. I'll go, Rosie.
I'll go.
(*To mike:*) I went to the front door and opened it.
The bolt fell off in my hand.
Two people were standing there in the mist.
A man and a woman.
The man said:

5

STANLEY. Oh.
We're your new neighbours.
We've come about the village fête.

NANCY. Sorry?

STANLEY. May we come in?

NANCY. Of course.
How rude of me.
I hope you'll excuse the mess.

STANLEY. Certainly.
May I introduce my wife?
This is my wife.
Her name's Janet.

JANET. How do you do.
My name's Janet.

NANCY. Yes.
My name's Nancy.
Nancy Empson.

STANLEY. Empson. Empson?
I know that name.
It's most unusual, isn't it?

NANCY. It is quite.

STANLEY. My name's Jones.
That's not an unusual name.
It's Welsh actually – in origin.

JANET. But we're not Welsh.

NANCY. Ah.

JANET. We're English.

NANCY. Yes. Good. Splendid.
Well, perhaps you'd like to come into the drawing-room and
I could offer you something.

STANLEY. No, no, we don't want to intrude.
It's just that we thought we'd come about the village fête.

NANCY. The village fête?

STANLEY. That's right.
It's at the end of the month.
We all take part in the village fête.
Well, it's expected from this end of the village.
We all run a stall, and we thought you'd like to decide which stall
you'd want to run.

NANCY. Yes, yes.
But it's rather inconvenient at the moment.
We've had a 22 per cent gas leak.
They've cut us off and condemned our boiler.
We haven't even started to unpack yet.
So . . . so it's rather inconvenient, you see.

STANLEY. I suppose it must be.

JANET. Moving into strange houses is always inconvenient, isn't it?
That's why Stanley and I don't move.
It's a matter of principle, isn't it, Stanley?

STANLEY. Quite right, Janet.
We are what I like to call 'stay putters'.
We've lived in this village for . . .
Empson?
Empson?
Got it.
Isn't it to do with writing?
Isn't there a famous writer called Empson?

NANCY. Well, there's the famous poet, William Empson.

STANLEY. William Empson!

That's it.
He's not a poet.
He writes books about railways
Are you by any chance related to him?

NANCY. Yes.
William is my brother.

STANLEY. Good gracious me.
How wonderful.
I am a train buff myself, you know.

NANCY. Really?

STANLEY. Oh yes.
I've got a library full of books about railways.
I've got every book that's ever been written by William Empson,
haven't I, Janet?

JANET. Oh yes.
And they're real dust hoarders, too.
Not just his books.
Everybody's books.
I wouldn't want to single him out.

STANLEY. I should say not.
William Empson!
I would go so far as to say that he's quite a hero of mine.

NANCY. In that case come and meet him.

STANLEY. He's . . . he's in this house?
Now?

NANCY. Oh yes.
Permanently.
He'll be living here.

STANLEY. Good gracious me.
What luck.
This is the happiest day of my life.

NANCY (*to mike*). I showed them into the drawing-room.
I introduced them to the family and found a tea chest for each of
them to sit on.
And soon William and Stanley were chatting happily.

6

STANLEY. I think the book I most admired of yours, William, if I
might call you William, of course.

WILLIAM. Yes, you may.

STANLEY. Thank you.
I think the book I most admired of yours was that lovely little
slim volume about the branch lines of the South Wales coalfield.

WILLIAM. Ah yes.
That was always a favourite of mine.

STANLEY. Mind you, I'd be hard pressed to set it before your
marvellous history of the London and North Western Railway.

WILLIAM. Yes.
A great favourite of mine, the London and North Western
Railway.

STANLEY. Mine, too.
Didn't they have the most wonderful locomotives?
I'm a particular fan of the George the Fifth class, 4-4-0.

WILLIAM. Ah yes.
Splendid engines.
They'd got Schmidt superheaters, you know.

STANLEY. Oh, I know, I know.

WILLIAM. They were based on the original Precursor design of
1904, you know.

STANLEY. Well, I never.
Isn't it amazing how you live and learn?

NANCY (*to mike*). They gossiped happily on about cylinders and
boiler pressures and valve diameters.
And we talked to Janet.

JANET. Well, of course, now you're living in the country you'll have
to realise that we don't get the services that you city slickers got
in the city.

ROSIE. We're hardly city slickers.

JANET. Yes, I know.
But you obviously expect to be able to pick up the phone and
everyone will come rushing out to you.
You want this attended to, you want that attended to, and out
they come at the drop of a hat.
Well, they don't here.

ROSIE. No, I don't suppose they do.

NANCY. What do they do, Janet?
What do you do, if anything goes wrong?

JANET. Oh, we ring for Winston.

ROSIE. Winston?

JANET. Yes, he's the local odd job man and poacher.
If you want any plumbing done, you call for Winston.

If you want a tree chopped down, you call for Winston.
If you want a salmon or a brace of pheasant, you call for Winston.
He's absolutely invaluable, is Winston.
We couldn't survive without him.

ROSIE. Then we'd better call up Winston, hadn't we?

NANCY (*to mike*) I called up Winston.
He arrived three days later.
Three days in which half the ceiling in the drawing-room fell down, in which we discovered half the sockets and switches in the house were live, in which we discovered the most disgusting smell in the downstairs loo, in which we . . . (*Bitter little laugh.*) . . . in which we discovered everything.
And Winston appeared.
He was a short, stocky man with long black hair falling over his shoulders.
He had a blue-veined chip between his two front teeth.
And he had one of those Zapata moustaches which wandered aimlessly at the tips and drooped into the stubble on his chin.
His shirt was open to the waist and he had a tattoo above each nipple.
Above his right nipple was tattooed the word 'Mild'.
Above his left nipple was tattooed the word 'Bitter'.
He smiled and stepped inside without being asked.

7

WINSTON. Ah yes, missus, I knows this house well.
Indeed I do.

NANCY. Oh, I see.
It has a history, has it?

WINSTON. I should say so, missus.
And so had its owner, old Wilson Rappaport.
You ever met him?

NANCY. No, he'd died two months before I came to view the house.

WINSTON. That was the worst thing you ever done in your life look.

NANCY. Pardon?

WINSTON. The worst thing you ever done in your life was to come down here and take over this house from Wilson Rappaport.
What a man he was.
A laugh.

A rogue and a vagabond.
Course he organised the village fête look.

NANCY. The village fête!
That's all I've heard since we moved in – the village fête.

WINSTON. Well, you would, missus.
The village fête?
It's the highlight of the year here.
And it's being held at the end of the month, you know.

NANCY. Yes, I have been made aware of that.

WINSTON. Good, good.
Just so long as you knows.
Are you going to keep the swimming pool in the back garden?

NANCY. No, I don't think so.

WINSTON. You do right, missus.
That swimming pool, he's a positive death trap, is that swimming pool look.
Full of germs from top to bottom.
Course old Wilson Rappaport, well, he looked after it proper.
Oh yes.
He heated it. He filtrated it. Course he didn't pay for nothing.

NANCY. No?

WINSTON. No.
He just by-passed the gas meter.
That's why you got all them pipes littered over your garden look.
No legality to them.
He botched them up hisself.

NANCY. That probably explains why we had a gas leak then.
Twenty-two per cent and rising.

WINSTON. Course it do.
And your electrics'll be up the spout, too.

NANCY. That's one of the things I want to see you about.

WINSTON. Yes.
I was waiting for you to call about them.
As soon as I knew new folk was moving in, I said to the missus:
'Won't be long before they call to ask about the electrics,' I ses.
And your roof needs doing, too.

NANCY. Not according to the surveyor.

WINSTON. Oh, you don't take no notice of surveyors, missus.
They don't know nothing round here look.
You get a surveyor in the city, and he knows something.
But you get a surveyor here and . . .
Do you know your extension's illegal?

NANCY. Pardon?

WINSTON. The extension at the back of your kitchen.
He's illegal.
Old Wilson Rappaport he never got no planning permission
for it.

NANCY. No?

WINSTON. No.
Not him.

NANCY. Is it important?

WINSTON. Course it's important, missus.
When you lives in the country, look, you has to have planning
permission for everything.
You has to have planning permission, if you wants to go and have
a shit.

NANCY. Thank you very much, Winston, but I don't think we'll
have language like that round this house, if you please.
Now then perhaps you'd like to have a look round and see what
needs doing and give us an estimate.

WINSTON. Oh I doesn't need to do that, missus.
I know what needs doing look.
See this meter here?
Well, he needs slinging straight away.
He's dangerous.
And he's illegal, too.
Now look at this rad here.
That's what we calls a radiator in the trade.
Well, he needs throwing out.
They all needs throwing out.
And your roof?
Well, he needs doing as I already said.
And your swimming pool needs going out.
Everything needs going out.
This house needs completely re-gutting from top to bottom.

NANCY. I have to tell you, Winston, that it wasn't my plan when we
moved here to have the house completely re-gutted.
The survey simply said it needed a certain amount of work doing.

WINSTON. Ah yes, missus, but what did they mean by 'a certain
amount of work'?
The word 'certain', he covers a multitude of sins.
Oh yes, he covers a multitude right enough.

NANCY (to mike). I began to show Winston around the house.
I knocked on the door of William's study and said:

8

NANCY (*to* WILLIAM). William, is it convenient if we come in for a minute?

WILLIAM (*from inside the study*). It's never convenient to come in when I'm working.

NANCY. But I've got the workman here, William.
He wants to see what needs doing.

WINSTON (*from inside the study*). OK, OK.
But make it quick.
I'm right in the middle of the section on marshalling yards. Get that wrong and I've lost the whole feel and voice of the book.
I've . . .
Oh, come on in. (*Opening the door.*)

NANCY. This is Winston.
Winston, this is my brother, William.

WINSTON. How do you do, sir.
Very pleasant to make your acquaintance.
My God, this room.

He sucks in his breath.

Oooh, he's in a state.

WILLIAM. What do you mean 'he's in a state'?

WINSTON. Well, look at your electrics.
They're a death-trap.

WILLIAM. What?

WINSTON. Yeah.
You put a plug in that socket and you'll go up like a Trident rocket.

WILLIAM. You mean it's dangerous?

WINSTON. Oh, to be sure.
I take this screwdriver look and stick it in that socket and what happens?

A loud bang.

Look at that.
If I didn't know what I was doing I'd have been a gonner by now.
Yeah, fried alive.

WILLIAM. Oh, my Lord.

9

NANCY (*to mike*). Winston smiled and sucked at the gap between his
two front teeth.
And we went inside into Rosie's room.
She was working at a drawing board:
She didn't hear us enter.
The sun was streaming in through the window and I must say she
looked quite lovely.
In her smock and her blonde hair tied at the nape picking out the
rays of the sun.
I said softly:
(*To* ROSIE:) Rosie.
Rosie, the workman's here.
(*To mike:*) And Rosie turned.
She smiled.
And I thought, what a beautiful woman she is when she smiles.
Why doesn't she smile more often?
Why doesn't she let herself go?

ROSIE. Hello.
I'm Rosie.

WINSTON. And I'm Winston.
Pleased to make your acquaintance.
That I am.
You a drawer by any chance?
You draw pictures?

ROSIE. No.
I make designs.

WINSTON. So do I, missus.
I've had designs on every young woman in this village look.
That I have and no mistake.

He laughs warmly.

NANCY (*to mike*). Then Rosie laughed, too.
They laughed together.

The sound of their laughter.

How strange that she should laugh with a complete stranger.
How very curious.

WINSTON. Well then, missus, the electrics are up the spout here
as well.
Same as all the house.
Tell you what I'll do.
I'll completely re-wire it for £874 inclusive of Vee Ay Tee and
VAT cash in hand.

NANCY. How much?

WINSTON. Well, you take it or leave it, missus.
I'm not hiding nothing from you.
He'll be a messy job.
But you do need your electrics doing urgent.
And your roof.

NANCY. I don't need the roof doing.

WINSTON. Well then, on your head be it, missus.
Same as that ceiling in your drawing-room.

NANCY. How do you know so much about this house, Winston?

WINSTON. Oh everyone knows this house look.
Everyone in the village.
Old Wilson Rappaport, he were a laugh.
He had everyone back here sooner or later.
He used to have these parties down by the swimming pool.
Oh yes, everyone in the village came.
They'd get tanked up after a sesh at the pub and they'd stagger
down here and they'd be jumping into the pool fully clothed and
some of them didn't have no clothes at all look.
Oh, he was a character, old Wilson Rappaport.
He ran the village fête, you know.

ROSIE. So we have been told.
Umpteen times.
Many many times.

WINSTON. Well, you would, miss, that's a fact.
You see old Wilson Rappaport what used to live in this house he
ran the whole caboodle.
And you'll be expected to do the same.

ROSIE. What?

WINSTON. Well, I reckons it's a bit of a tradition in the
village look.
Them what lives in this house has to organise the village fête.

NANCY. Not any more, Winston.
Not any more.
We refuse categorically to have anything to do with the
village fête.
And that is our final word on the subject.

10

*The clacking of a typewriter and then the sudden noise of a sledge-hammer being
applied to a wall.*

WINSTON. Not disturbing you, am I, William?

WILLIAM (*painfully*). No, you're not disturbing me, Winston.
I'm only trying to write the penultimate chapter of my book.
Nothing important.

WINSTON. Oh good.
I don't know how you writers manage to write with all this noise
and disturbance going on.
Can you write when people are talking to you?

WILLIAM. With great difficulty, Winston.
With enormous difficulty.

WINSTON. Well, that's just like me look.
When I'm knocking a wall down or drilling an hole, I can work
and talk at the same time. But I'm damned if I can go down the
pub and play a game of darts and talk at the same time.
I expect that's just like you, is it, William?

WILLIAM. Well, sort of, yes.

WINSTON. What do you write books about then?
Dirty things?

WILLIAM. I beg your pardon?

WINSTON. You know.
Do you write them smutty things about Hollywood?

WILLIAM. No.
No, I write about railways.

WINSTON. Oh well, you can get up to some rare old dirty things on
railways, can't you?
I remember last time I went cross to Yeovil the day after the
village fête.
I went with Betty Hayball. Cor!
You know Betty Hayball, eh?

WILLIAM. No, I can't say I do.

WINSTON. You not met Betty Hayball yet?
Well, you got a nice surprise coming to you, and that's a fact.
She's what I calls nice and juicy and ripe, if you follows my
meaning as regards her endowments.
She's my first cousin, too.
Well, there we are together in this empty compartment look,
going cross to Yeovil and . . .

WILLIAM. That used to be on the Somerset and Dorset line.

WINSTON. What?

WILLIAM. Yeovil.
It used to be on the Somerset and Dorset line.
They called it the Somerset and Dorset Committee.
I'm writing a book about it.

WINSTON. A serious book?

WILLIAM. Yes.

WINSTON. You're writing a serious book about railways?

WILLIAM. Yes.
That's what I do.

WINSTON. And they ain't smutty?

WILLIAM. Oh no.

WINSTON. Ah.
Well, that explains a lot, William.
That do explain a lot look.

The hammering resumes and so does the typewriting.

NANCY (*to mike*). The banging and hammering and drilling went on for days and days.
And William did not once complain.
How strange.
How very curious.
Meanwhile Father established himself in his shed and was very happy.
Not a word of complaint.
How strange.
How curious.
Of course he'd secured his supplies of gin.
From Stanley.
We weren't supposed to know.
But we did.
Every house we moved from we'd find this great cache of empty gin bottles and Father would say:
'Goodness, me, I wonder how they got there?'
Yes. Mm.
Things couldn't be all that strange, if Father were still tippling at his gin.

11

Garden noises.

FATHER. Nancy, Nancy.

NANCY. Yes, Father?

FATHER. Are we going to keep this swimming pool?

NANCY. I don't know.
Why do you ask?

FATHER. Well, you know that wallah who's knocking holes in the walls and doing things to the house?

NANCY. Winston.

FATHER. That's him – Winston.
Well, he was telling me yesterday that this pond is very probably a breeding ground for malaria and beriberi.

NANCY. Really, Father?

FATHER. Yes.
It reminds me very much of a stagnant pond I once knew when I went to India with your mother.
We were staying in this rest house.
Up in the hills.
Or was it the plains?
I don't remember.
But there was a stagnant pond there and this fearfully pleasant old Indian cove came up to me and doffed his panama and said:
'No goee into pondee, Sahib.'
And I said:
'No?
'And why not, old chap?'
And he said:
'Very very bad diseases there, Sahib.'
And I said:
'Oh?
'Malaria?'
And he said:
'Yes.'
Very interesting conversation that was. Nancy.
Didn't speak to him again.
Pity.
I rather regretted that.
I felt that we had a certain something between us.
Don't you think so?

The noise of a helicopter.

I say, another helicopter.
This really is a very very pleasant spot you've dragged us to,
Nancy.
Fearfully pleasant.

NANCY (*to mike*). And he pottered off happily to his shed.
Not a word of complaint about his legs, or his sinus, or his chest.
I don't know why, but for a moment my whole body shivered.
I felt that someone was watching me.
I felt that someone was standing right behind me.
I turned.
There was no one there.

But I felt a draught and although there was no breeze the spider's
web on the standard rose swayed backwards and forwards.
Backwards and forwards.

The noise of the helicopter again.

It took Winston five days to rewire the house.
He said it would take another three to make good, as he put it.
There was still no boiler, though.
And we had to heat our water for washing and bathing in an old
copper cauldron.
But not a word of complaint did we hear from Rosie.
Not once did I have to calm or placate her.
She was coping.
And so was William.
He came into the drawing-room one Friday evening.
And he looked very smug and very contented.

12

WILLIAM. I've finished the book.
I think it's my best yet.

ROSIE. I'm very pleased for you, William.
I'm thrilled.

NANCY. There's no need to be sarcastic, Rosie.

ROSIE. I'm not being sarcastic.
I mean it.
It's the same with me.
I'm producing the best designs I've ever done in my life.

WILLIAM. I think it must be the house.
I really like it here.

NANCY. What?
You like the house?

WILLIAM. Yes, it's got a certain ambience about it, which makes me
feel comfortable and at ease.

ROSIE. And creative.

WILLIAM. Yes.
Creative.

FATHER. Happy, too.

NANCY. What?

FATHER. Happy, Nancy.
I think we're all happy, don't you?

NANCY. Happy?
　　You, happy?
　　I'm not listening to this nonsense a moment longer.
　　I'm going to the kitchen to make cocoa for Father.
　　(*To mike:*) Happy?
　　At ease with the world?
　　What's come over them?
　　They've never been happy and contented and at ease with
　　the world.
　　Never never wherever we've lived.
　　They've always quarrelled and complained and . . .
　　If they're happy, where do I fit in?
　　What role do I have to play in their lives?
　　What role do I have to play in my own life?

Pause.

13

Then ring at front door.

NANCY (*shouting*). I'll answer it.
　　I'll go.
　　You get on with being happy.

Footsteps to the front door. The door opens.

　　Oh, Stanley.
　　Janet.

STANLEY. Hello.
　　Nice to see you again.
　　And I'm sure Janet feels the same way, too.

JANET. Oh yes.
　　It's really nice to see you.
　　And William and Stanley have become such good friends, haven't
　　you, Stanley?

STANLEY. Oh yes.
　　And so have your Father and I.
　　He's got an endless fund of fascinating stories about India,
　　you know.

NANCY. I know.

STANLEY. Yes.
　　I wonder if I could introduce you to Mrs Godwin.
　　She's the lady who's standing on my left.
　　The opposite side to Janet.
　　She's standing on my right hand side.

NANCY. How do you do, Mrs Godwin.
My name's Nancy Empson.

MRS GODWIN. How do you do.
I've heard a lot about your brother and sister and father from
Stanley here.
I'm longing to meet them.

NANCY. Then may I invite you inside and offer you a drink?
You won't find them a nuisance.

MRS GODWIN. I'm sure I shan't.

NANCY (*to mike*). She stepped inside with Stanley and Janet.
She was a tall and elegant woman.
In fact, she was very tall, and she was very elegant.
She wore those dungarees.
Pink with leather boots.
And she had deep auburn hair in a frizzy perm like the one I had
done in Southwold, which didn't suit me.
Her fingernails were long and they were painted carmine.
I introduced her to my family and when she looked at William,
he blushed.

MRS GODWIN. It's a great pleasure to meet you, William.
Stanley's told me such a lot about you.
He lent me one of your books.

WILLIAM. Oh yes?
Which one?

MRS GODWIN. I can't quite remember.
I think it was about railways.

STANLEY. Yes, well, yes, I took the liberty of inviting Mrs Godwin
over here because she's what I call quite a big cheese as regards
the village fête.

NANCY. The village fête!
Not that again?

MRS GODWIN. Don't you like village fêtes?

NANCY. No, we do not, do we, Rosie?

ROSIE. Oh, I don't know.

NANCY. What?
What's that you say?

MRS GODWIN. Well, if you're not sure, perhaps you'd like to
come to one of my parties.
We have some lovely parties.
They're quite well known in the village, aren't they, Stanley?

STANLEY. Yes.
Yes, they are, although I hasten to add that Janet and I do not

partake of them very frequently, do we, Janet?

JANET. No.
We're more of the stay-at-home type.

MRS GODWIN. I know.
But perhaps William or Rosie or even Nancy might like to come
to one of our parties.

ROSIE. That would be nice.
Thank you.

MRS GODWIN. I'm sure you'd enjoy them.
They're very entertaining.
Quite novel really.

FATHER. I like novel parties.
I once went to a frightfully modern party.
In India.
With your mother.
It was in Goa.

STANLEY. Goa, eh?

FATHER. Yes.
The little black blighters who live there are Roman Catholics, you
know. It's odd seeing that.
You don't expect to find Roman Catholics in India, do you?
Muslims, yes, Hindus, Buddhists, Parsees, cricketers.
India's produced the most wonderful crop of cricketers in
its time.
Engineer, Merchant, Contractor.
Curious how their surnames are the names of trades and
professions.
Though I don't ever recall an Indian test cricketer called
Furniture Remover or . . .
I once saw the Indians play at Sevenoaks – or was it Eastbourne?

WILLIAM. Maidstone.

FATHER. I beg your pardon, William?

WILLIAM. You saw them play at Maidstone, Father.
The Nawab of Pataudi scored seven.

FATHER. Really?
How lovely for him.
Er . . . er . . . Where was I?

NANCY. Goa, Father.
You were in Goa.

FATHER. Yes, yes, so I was.
Well, there we were in Goa, your mother and I and this chappie
who made hat stands out of balsa wood.
Don't ask me why. I suppose some people do. And some people

don't.
Anyway, there we were and . . . he scored eleven.

NANCY. Who, Father? Who?

FATHER. The Nawab of Pataudi.
He had the most exquisite range of strokes on the off side.
I wonder if he liked curry.
Yes. Well . . . there we were on Ascension Day.
Or was it Shrove Tuesday?
It doesn't matter, I suppose.
Anyway at this party they . . .

14

NANCY (*to mike, almost screaming*). I hate parties.
I hate them, I hate them.
And I hate village fêtes, too.

The noise of hammering and typewriter. The hammering stops.

WINSTON. I hear tell that Mrs Godwin visited you last night,
William.

The typewriter stops.

WILLIAM. What?

WINSTON. That Mrs Godwin.
You know, the good-looker with the big tits.

WILLIAM. I don't think I noticed them.

WINSTON. What?
You didn't notice them?
Everyone else has a look.
Oooh, I could tell you a thing or two about Mrs Godwin.
She's the organiser in chief of all the village wife-swapping in the
village, she is.

WILLIAM. Wife-swapping?

WINSTON. Wife-swapping.
It's rampant in the country, is wife-swapping.
Not among us class of course.
But among you lot at this end of the village it's endemic look.
And them mucky videos what you plays on the telly.

WILLIAM. What?

WINSTON. There's no need to look so surprised, William.
This is the country.
It ain't the city.
Last year . . . ooooh . . . last year within a radius of thirty odd

miles of here we had two cases of murder, five rapes and God
knows how many outbreaks of arson.
It's quite a speciality arson in these parts look.
You'll love it once you gets used to it.

WILLIAM. Will I?

WINSTON. Course you will.
Specially when that Mrs Godwin gets her hands on you.

WILLIAM. What?

WINSTON. That's why she come round, William.
To lay claim on you.

WILLIAM. What?

WINSTON. Well, she had old Wilson Rappaport.
So now he's snuffed it she's going to take you.
You comes with the house.

WILLIAM. I come with the house?

WINSTON. Yes.
She was always round here, that Mrs Godwin.
Her and old Wilson Rappaport cavorting?
Cor I could tell you some tales.
And talking about that, you knows your sister?

WILLIAM. Which one?

WINSTON. That Rosie.

WILLIAM. Yes?
What about her?

WINSTON. Is she courting?

WILLIAM. Pardon?

WINSTON. Has she got a gentleman friend?

WILLIAM. No.
No, she hasn't.

WINSTON. We'll soon see about that then.
I will introduce myself to her tonight all dicky dolled up and
respectable and ask her if she would like to accompany me on a
sesh at the pub.

WILLIAM. But I thought you were married.

WINSTON. Course I'm married.
What's that got to do with it?

WILLIAM. But Rosie isn't like that.
She wouldn't dream of going out with a married man.

WINSTON. Ah, don't you be so daft look.
This is the country.

You're living in the country now, William.
You got to settle into our ways, ain't you?

NANCY (*to mike*). That night around half past six there was a ring at
the front door.
I answered it.
And there was Winston.
I don't think I'd ever had such a surprise in the whole of my life.
He was wearing a navy blue corduroy suit.
And it was very well cut.
He was wearing a pink shirt.
And that was very well cut, too.
And he had a canary yellow cravat with red fox heads on it.
His hair was combed back.
The stubble on his chin had been shaved away.
And he smelled of rather expensive perfume.

WINSTON. I just called on the off-chance, missus.

NANCY. On the off-chance, Winston?

WINSTON. That's right.
I called on the off-chance that your sister, Rosie, might like to go
out with me this evening in my car, in my motor look.

NANCY. Rosie?
Rosie go out with you?

WINSTON. Yes, why not?
I'll show her a bit of the countryside, look.
Show her around.
Show her some nice places off of the beaten track.
A young girl like her, well, it's not right she should be stuck on
her own in a rat-trap of a place like this all night long.
Bloody damp – she'll catch her death of cold.
And that's another thing, missus.
You need your damp courses doing.
I'll start on that day after tomorrow when I've finished with your
rads look.

NANCY (*to mike:*) I could hardly believe what I was hearing.
I could hardly believe what I was seeing.
And I could hardly believe myself when I turned and shouted:
(*To* ROSIE:) Rosie, Rosie.

ROSIE (*calling from the back of the house*). What is it?

NANCY. There's someone to see you.

ROSIE (*calling*). I'm busy.

NANCY. That is not my concern, Rosie.
You can please yourself.
All I am saying is that there is someone to see you.

ROSIE. Blast!

Her approaching footsteps.

Who is it?
What do they . . .
Winston!
Winston, is it you?

WINSTON. That's right, Rosie.

ROSIE. And you've come to visit me?

WINSTON. Yes.
I thought you might like to go out for a sesh.
In the car.
In the motor.
It's a blue one.
Very comfy. Very agreeable.
Good engine.
Classy upholstery.
Got it for seventy-two quid from old Jim Filbert with the cast in
his right eye.
Right then, Rosie.
Put your coat on, and we'll go.

NANCY (*to mike*). And to my amazement, to my profound
astonishment, she went.
She went off with Winston.
And she was smiling.
And she let him hold her hand as she climbed into the car.
And as it pulled away from the house she waved at me.
And she blew me a kiss.
And as the car disappeared from view I felt that feeling again.
Someone was watching me.
Someone was laughing at me.
I turned.
I spun round quickly.
But there was no one there.

15

Pub noises. There's a guitarist singing bad country and western music.

ROSIE. Who on earth is that awful man singing?

WINSTON. Oh, ignore him, silly old sod.
He works down the abattoir.
Can't you tell by the way he sings?

ROSIE *laughs.*

You not got a regular bloke then, Rosie?

ROSIE. No, I haven't as a matter of fact.

WINSTON. Have you ever had a regular bloke?

ROSIE. Oh yes.

WINSTON. Was he a nice bloke?

ROSIE. I thought so.

WINSTON. What did he do then, this bloke of yours?

ROSIE. He was a pilot.
In the RAF.

WINSTON. Oh.
He flew aeroplanes, did he?

ROSIE. Yes.
He crashed and got killed.

WINSTON. Ah.
Happens to the best of them, Rosie.
Happens to the best of them look.
Them boys, they go up in them planes, and half the time they
don't know what's what, do they?

ROSIE. No they don't, Winston.
No, they don't.

WINSTON. Still, no use crying over spilled milk, Rosie.
You got me now.
Well, you got me for this evening, ain't you?

ROSIE (*laughs*). Yes, I have.
Won't your wife be alarmed?

WINSTON. No, she's used to it, Rosie.
She don't mind me having a bit of fluff on the side.

ROSIE. A bit of fluff?

WINSTON. Yes, a bit of fluff.
Well, makes marriage a damn sight more interesting, that's what
I think.
I wouldn't mind if she had her own bit of spare on the side.
She wants to, too.
Trouble is she's so bloody ugly no one'll look at her.
More's the pity, eh?
Wish I'd married a beautiful woman like you, Rosie.

ROSIE. Pardon?

WINSTON. I could have gone my way.
You could have gone yours.
Would have made all the difference in the world to the
marriage look.

ROSIE. Yes, yes.
   Have you got any children, Winston?

WINSTON. Eight.

ROSIE. Eight?

WINSTON. That's right.
   And another on the way.
   All as ugly as her every one of them.
   Like peas in a pod they are.

ROSIE. Have you lived here all your life?

WINSTON. Oh yes, I lived here all my life.
   All my life I has.

ROSIE. Do you like it here?

WINSTON. Well, I don't know nothing different, do I, Rosie?

ROSIE. No.
   You're quite lucky really.

WINSTON. Course I am.
   Listen, every morning I gets up at five in the morning.
   And in the summer and spring I goes down to the bottom of my
   garden and there's a wood there.
   A little wood look.
   And I goes deep inside and I hears the birds singing.
   Chiff chaffs, warblers, nightjars churring away.
   And I sits down with my back against this old beech tree and
   I listens to them.
   And I thinks to myself:
   You're dead lucky, you little buggers.
   If you was any bigger I'd shoot you with my shot gun quick as
   look at you and have you in my stock pot.

ROSIE (*laughs*). Winston!

WINSTON. Yes.
   Then I goes back inside, and I has my breakfast.
   A slice of dripping toast and a glass of port.

ROSIE. A glass of port for breakfast?

WINSTON. To be sure, yes.
   A slice of dripping toast and a glass of port for breakfast – do you
   all the good in the world, Rosie. You wants to try it.
   Build you up.
   Put a bit of flesh on you.
   A bit more flesh on you up top, my dear, and you'd be the apple
   of my eye.

ROSIE. Well, I might just try it, Winston.

WINSTON. Yes, of course you should.

All my bits of fluff, they all has a bit of the old dripping toast
and port.
Well, they wants to keep well in with old Winston, don't they?

ROSIE. I suppose they do, Winston.
You're quite a singular man after all.

WINSTON. Oh yes.
That I am, to be sure.
Can I tell you something, Rosie?
Something personal?

ROSIE. Yes.
What is it?

WINSTON. You ain't got no stench pipe.

ROSIE. What?

WINSTON. You ain't got no stench pipe.
At the back of your house.
Old Wilson Rappaport, he took it down.
Why, I do not know.
Tell you what, though, Rosie.

ROSIE. What?

WINSTON. I'll put you one in.
Free and gratis.
Just for you, Rosie.
Free and gratis.

ROSIE. Thank you, Winston.
You've made the evening so much worthwhile.

WINSTON. Yes, well, I always like to look after my bits of fluff,
don't I?
You want another beer?

ROSIE. No.
I don't drink beer.
I'm drinking gin and tonic.

WINSTON. Well, you don't want no more of them then.
Make you pee all night, won't it?
Come on, I'll take you home.

ROSIE. But it's only half past eight.

WINSTON. Course it is, Rosie.
But I got up early in the morning, ain't I?
Five o'clock.
Come on, let's be off then.
Tell you what, though, Rosie.

ROSIE. What's that?

WINSTON. You give me a kiss when I drops you at your front door

and I'll get you a new gas boiler.
Free and gratis.
Yes.
Give us a kiss and you can have a new gas boiler.
Free and gratis with no payment required.

16

NANCY (*to mike*). Next morning Winston arrived with a new
gas boiler.
And he put it in.
And he didn't charge us.
He said it was free and gratis.
And he smiled and winked.
And Rosie smiled, too.
What on earth was going on?
Smiling faces and laughter.
And in the afternoon William with a spring to his step and a
sparkle in his eyes saying:

WILLIAM. I'm just going out, Nancy.

NANCY. Oh fine.
Going for a walk, are you?
Going to meet Stanley?

WILLIAM. No.
No, as a matter of fact I'm going visiting.

NANCY. Oh, that's nice.
You've made a chum.

WILLIAM. Yes.

NANCY. Anyone I know?

WILLIAM (*coughs nervously*). Yes.
Yes, it's . . . it's Mrs Godwin.

NANCY. Mrs Godwin?

WILLIAM. Yes.
She's . . . she's asked me round to tea.
I'm taking her one of my books.
A potted history of the L.N.E.R.
Cheery bye then.

NANCY (*to mike*). And off he went.
With a spring to his step and a sparkle in his eye.
What was happening?
What was happening to us all?

17

The sound of drinks and tea things.

MRS GODWIN. Would you care for something a little stronger
than tea, William?

WILLIAM. Oh no.
Not at four o'clock in the afternoon, Mrs Godwin.

MRS GODWIN. I'd much rather you called me Lucy.

WILLIAM. Certainly.
Only too happy, Lucy.

MRS GODWIN. Are you well ahead with your preparations for the
village fête, William?

WILLIAM. No.
No, I don't go in for things like that.
None of the family does.
We're very private people, you see.

MRS GODWIN. But it's expected of you.

WILLIAM. Yes, I rather gathered that.

MRS GODWIN. It's expected of the house.
Mr Rappaport virtually organised the whole village fête himself.

WILLIAM. Yes, but I'm not like Mr Rappaport.

MRS GODWIN. No?

WILLIAM. No.

MRS GODWIN. In what way are you different from Wilson,
Mr Rappaport?

WILLIAM. I . . . I . . . like to keep myself to myself.
I like my own company.
Well, present company excepted, of course.

MRS GODWIN. Are you a single man, William?

WILLIAM. Yes.
I always have been.
All my life.
I always will be, I suppose.

MRS GODWIN. And why is that?

WILLIAM. I don't seem to have time for it.
I'm very busy with my books, you see.

MRS GODWIN. Ah.

WILLIAM. What people don't realise is that it's not only the writing
of the book which takes up your time.
It's also the research.

There's a great deal of research to be done.
Before I start writing a book I always do my research in loco
and . . .

He laughs.

In loco?
That's not a bad joke for someone who writes books about
railways, is it?

MRS GODWIN. It's very good.

Pause.

Do you like village life, William?

WILLIAM. I must say I do really.
I didn't at first.

MRS GODWIN. No?

WILLIAM. No.
You see I didn't want to come here.
And neither did Rosie, if the truth be known.
We came because of Father.
His chest.
We always seem to be moving because of Father.
We lived at the seaside and had to leave because of his sinus.
We lived in the North Country and had to leave because of
his legs.

MRS GODWIN. His legs?

WILLIAM. All those hills.
He couldn't get up them.
Which was rather a pity because we lived on top of a hill, you see.

MRS GODWIN. And what about Nancy?

WILLIAM. Nancy?

MRS GODWIN. Nancy.
How does she fit in?
Does she like moving?

WILLIAM. Oh no, she . . .
It's strange you should say that.

MRS GODWIN. Why?

WILLIAM. Well, until we moved here I always thought she hated
moving as much as Rosie and I did.
And then . . .
Well, I looked at her the other day and it suddenly came over me.
I thought you liked all this moving, Nancy.
Deep down you really liked it.

MRS GODWIN. Why did you think that, William?

WILLIAM. I don't know.
It's just a feeling I had that she likes to keep us on our toes.
Keep us from settling in.
Keep us from being happy.
Because when we're not happy, she takes charge.
She's the boss.
She has a role to play.
And now we're happy and contented here, she's not wanted.
She's not needed.
She's . . .
Oh, that's a dreadful thing to say.
I'm sorry.
It's very disloyal of me.
And yet.
And yet.

Pause.

MRS GODWIN. I wonder if you'd like to come to one of my parties, William.

WILLIAM. Pardon?

MRS GODWIN. I'm giving a party tonight.

WILLIAM. Tonight?

MRS GODWIN. Yes.
An impromptu party.

WILLIAM. Will Stanley and Janet be here?

MRS GODWIN. No.

WILLIAM. Oh.
Will there by anyone I know at the party?

MRS GODWIN. Yes.

WILLIAM. Who?

MRS GODWIN. I'll be here.
Just me.

WILLIAM. Just you?
Just you on your own?

MRS GODWIN. Yes.
Just me.
On my own.
Do come round, William.
About eight o'clock would be lovely.
You can explain all the finer points of the book you've brought to me.
Finer points?
That's a good joke about a book on railways, isn't it?

18

The noise of a helicopter.

WILLIAM (*at the top of his voice*). I like it here.
  I love it here.

NANCY. William, for Heaven's sake, what's the matter with you?
  Dancing round like that and you're still wearing your pyjama
  jacket.

WILLIAM. I don't care.
  I'm happy, Nancy.
  Happy.
  I've never been so happy in the whole of my life.
  It's wonderful here.
  Absolutely wonderful.

FATHER. Yes.
  I think it's wonderful too.

NANCY. You, Father?

FATHER. Yes.
  Sleeping fearfully well since we moved here.
  Never slept better.
  Didn't sleep too well last night, mind you.
  You came home very late, William.
  You were whistling as you went upstairs.

WILLIAM. Was I?

NANCY. Were you?
  I didn't hear you come back.
  It must have been very late, William.
  Where had you been?

WILLIAM. Er . . . er . . . just down to the pub.
  Yes, to the pub.
  Meeting people.
  Talking about arrangements for the village fête.

NANCY. The village fête?

WILLIAM. Yes.
  It's expected of us, Nancy.
  And there's not long to go now, you know.

NANCY. But we're not having anything to do with the village fête.
  We decided that.

ROSIE. Oh, I don't think we decided it absolutely, did we, Nancy?

NANCY. What?

ROSIE. I think we should make the effort.
  As a matter of fact I've volunteered to help Winston on the

hoopla for the pig stall.

NANCY. Hoopla for the pig?
      You?
      Making a fool of yourself like that?

ROSIE. Why not?

WILLIAM. Exactly.
      Why not?
      I've sort of volunteered to help Mrs Godwin actually.

NANCY. Mrs Godwin?

WILLIAM. Yes.
      On the bring and buy stall.
      I thought I'd donate a couple of books.
      And Mrs Godwin suggested I stay there and volunteer to
      autograph them.
      It should be fun.
      I can help out.

FATHER. Yes, I think I might potter down there, too.
      Could always make myself useful if I don't get in the way.
      I remember going to a bazaar once.
      In India.
      With your mother.
      And there was a stall selling . . .

NANCY. Yes, Father.
      Yes, yes, yes.
      We've heard that story before.
      Many times.
      Many, many times.

ROSIE. There's no need to snap at Father like that.

NANCY. I'm not snapping.

ROSIE. Yes you are.
      I used to be an expert at snapping.
      And I know when people are snapping.

NANCY. Used to be?
      Used to be?
      Oh dear.
      Oh dear oh dear.

WILLIAM. Are you all right, Nancy?

NANCY. I don't know.
      I feel a little strange.
      I think I'm all right.
      But I'm not quite sure.
      (*To mike:*) I went into the little sitting-room I'd turned into a
      sewing-room for myself.

I sat down.
It was nice and quiet.
It was peaceful.
And then I had that strange feeling again.
I was being watched.
Someone was laughing at me.
Two people were laughing at me.
A man and a woman.
They were watching me and laughing at me.
And I was just about to scream at the top of my voice when . . .

19

The sound of the door being burst open.

WINSTON. Not disturbing you, am I, missus?

NANCY. Winston!
Oh, Winston, I've just had the most horrible . . .

She composes herself.

What do you want?

WINSTON. It's about your skirting board, missus.
It'll have to come up.
If I'm to put a new rad in, I've got to rip up your skirting board to
get at the pipes look.

NANCY. I didn't say anything about doing the rads.

WINSTON. Oh yes, you did, missus.
It was all included in that new estimate I give you the other day.
Put new rads in and make good look.

NANCY. I see.
I must have got it wrong.

WINSTON. Not to worry.
It's no crime getting things wrong.
It's . . .
You're looking a bit pale, missus, if you don't mind me saying so.
Is this country air not agreeing with you?

NANCY. Yes.
Yes, it is agreeing with me.
I suppose.
Although on the other hand I . . . I . . .

WINSTON. You wants to let yourself go, my dear, if you don't
mind me saying so.
You got to join in look.

You lives in the country, and you has to join in.
You can't be private and keep yourself to yourself.
Folks don't like it.
Neither does the birds and the flowers and the chalk streams and
the downlands.
Look at me.
I joins in.
But you know what I am basically, deep down by trade and by
inclination?

NANCY. No.

WINSTON. I'm a philosopher.

NANCY. A philosopher?

WINSTON. Oh yes.
I read all the books about it.
I'm a great reader look.
I read all the books about everything.
I read books by people you never heard of.
Jean Jacques Rousseau.
He's someone you never heard of.

NANCY. Well, as a matter of fact, Winston, I have heard of him.

WINSTON. Well then, that just shows what a lot we got in
common, don't it?

NANCY. What?

WINSTON. I've been watching you, Nancy.

NANCY. Watching me?

WINSTON. Yes.
You hasn't seen me.
You hasn't noticed.
But I been watching you.
And I been thinking.

NANCY. What have you been thinking?

WINSTON (*laughs*). Oooh, that'd be telling, wouldn't it, Nancy?
And blokes like me don't tell much to women.
Maybe to their bits of fluff.

NANCY. Bits of fluff?

WINSTON. Oh yes.
I tells my bits of fluff things from time to time.

NANCY. You've got bits of fluff?

WINSTON. Course I has.
That's why I don't practise being a philosopher.

NANCY. I don't follow.

WINSTON. It's simple, Nancy.
  There's no money to be earned round here being a philosopher.
  If you wants to earn money you got to chop down trees and do
  re-wiring and turn your hand to anything what people wants.
  That's the way to earn money.
  And you got to have money if you wants to buy presents for your
  bits of fluff, hasn't you?

NANCY. I suppose you do.
  And what sort of presents do you buy for your bits of
  fluff, Winston?

WINSTON. Oh this and that.
  A stench pipe here.
  A gas boiler there.
  You're not wanting anything for the house by any chance, are
  you, Nancy?

20

Pub noises again.

ROSIE. I'm getting to like this place, Winston.

WINSTON. Yes.
  It's all right.
  Fine place this.
  Well, a bloke can bring his bit of fluff on the side and no
  one notices.
  You go into the village pub and everyone knows.
  They all starts gossiping.
  Like what they're gossiping about your brother.

ROSIE. What are they gossiping about my brother?

WINSTON. Him and that Mrs Godwin.

ROSIE. What?

WINSTON. Didn't you know?
  They're having a bit of a fling.

ROSIE. William is having a fling with a married woman?

WINSTON. Yes.
  Well, they all does sooner or later.
  Hope he don't go the same way as old Wilson Rappaport.

ROSIE. Pardon?

WINSTON. Well, old Wilson he had a fling with that Mrs Godwin.
  That's why he committed suicide look.
  In that shed at the bottom of your garden.

ROSIE. What?

WINSTON. They found him there the day before the village fête.
  He'd done himself in.
  They reckoned it was because Mrs Godwin had give him
  the elbow.
  Hope William don't go the same way, eh Rosie?

ROSIE. William and Mrs Godwin.
  Who would have believed it?
  After all these years.
  And a beautiful woman, too.
  An elegant woman.
  What's happening?
  What's happening to us, Winston?

WINSTON. Don't you know, Rosie?

ROSIE. No.

WINSTON. It's the house, Rosie.
  It's your new house.

ROSIE. Yes.
  Yes, it's the house.
  There's this strange feeling of excitement, of danger, of . . .
  Winston.

WINSTON. Yes, Rosie?

ROSIE. Would you like to put up a picture rail in my workroom?

WINSTON. Free and gratis, Rosie?

ROSIE. Oh yes, Winston.
  Free and gratis.

NANCY (*to mike*). I'd never been so surprised in the whole of
  my life.
  A navy blue corduroy suit.
  A pink shirt.
  A yellow cravat with red foxes' heads.
  One day it rained.
  It didn't bother him.
  He sat high on the ridge of the roof and took his shirt off and the
  rain cascaded down his chest and the wind blew back his hair
  and . . .
  God, what's happening to me?
  That disgusting little man with his tattoos and his stubble and
  his . . .
  All the time I was being watched.
  In every part of the house I was being watched.
  Someone was there.
  Watching me, stalking me.

And then . . .
And then they held a committee meeting.
In our house.
About the village fête.
They actually held a committee meeting, and they didn't tell me
about it.

21

Committee meeting sounds.

WILLIAM. Well, everyone, as your chairman may I say that it is very
nice to see you all here tonight.
Lucy particularly.
Although that doesn't of course preclude Janet, Stanley, Rosie
and Winston.

WINSTON. Hear hear.
Now get on with it.

WILLIAM. Yes.
Well, we have apologies from Freddie Hayball, who can't be
present owing to personal bereavement in the family.

WINSTON. Personal bereavement?
Rubbish.
I knows all about Freddie Hayball.
He's my first cousin.
He'll be nicking from the abbatoir.
It's his night for it.
He'll be there with old Jim Filbert and they'll be . . .

ROSIE. Winston!

WINSTON. Sorry, Rosie.
Carry on, William.

WILLIAM. Yes.
Thank you.
And we have apologies from the Colonel who can't be here owing
to Peeping Toms in the neighbourhood.
Now then to summarise so far.
The village fête, as you know, is in ten days' time and everything
seems to be in order.
The stalls have been allocated, Winston is to cut the grass on the
meadow on the morning of the fête, the Salvation Army Band has
been booked and the Boys' Brigade will be doing their usual
demonstration.
I believe it's their usual demonstration, isn't it, Lucy?

MRS GODWIN. That's right, William.
  Their usual demonstration of the things boys get up to.

WINSTON. Hear hear.
  And so hurry up, William.
  I don't want to miss out on my sesh at the pub tonight.

WILLIAM. Sorry.
  Well, I've instructed the Fire Brigade to stand by and . . .

The door opens.

FATHER. Not barging in on anything important, am I?

ROSIE. As a matter of fact, you are, Father.
  We're holding a committee meeting.

FATHER. Oh, a committee meeting.
  I like committee meetings.
  Very fond of them.
  When I was in India with your mother we used to have any
  number of committee meetings.
  Yes, I'll never forget them.
  Can't remember what they were about, but they were most
  fearfully interesting.
  I remember this wallah with the big ears and the . . .

WINSTON begins to laugh.

  . . . or was it the other wallah with the cracked monocle and . . .

ROSIE joins in the laughter with WINSTON, so do the others.
The laughter grows louder and louder. Then fade to NANCY's point of
hearing as she sits in her sewing-room.

NANCY (*to mike*). They're laughing.
  Why are they laughing?
  We've never had laughter in our houses before.
  Never ever.
  Our houses have always been noted for their lack of laughter.
  What's going on?
  What on earth is going wrong with this family?
  What's going wrong with me?
  That disgusting little man with the Zapata moustache and the
  stubble on his chin will be sitting in my drawing-room, scuffing
  his boots on my carpet, dropping his cigarette ash on my sofa,
  spitting into the fireplace, wiping his nose on the . . . on the . . .
  I can't cope.
  I can't cope. I cannot cope.

She screams that last word. Silence. Then quietly and efficiently:

  I got up early next morning.
  I wanted to be on my own.
  But when I went into the kitchen, there was Rosie eating breakfast.

22

ROSIE. Hello, Nancy.
You're up early.

NANCY. Yes, I thought I'd . . .
What on earth are you eating?

ROSIE. Dripping toast.

NANCY. Dripping toast?
And you're drinking wine.

ROSIE. Port wine.
It's lovely.
You want to try it.
Put a bit of flesh on you, Nancy.
Make you rich and juicy and all desirable.

23

NANCY (*to mike*). I went out into the garden and there was William
in his pyjamas waving his arms and dancing round with a broom
clutched tightly to his chest.
(*To* WILLIAM:) William, what on earth are you doing?

WILLIAM. I'm happy, Nancy.
I'm glad to be alive.
Isn't it wonderful here?
Isn't it lovely to live in this village being committed, being an
integral part of the community?
That's what Lucy says, anyway, and I agree with her wholeheartedly.

NANCY. William.

WILLIAM. Yes, Nancy?

NANCY. You're not writing, are you?

WILLIAM. Oh yes, I am.

NANCY. What are you writing?

WILLIAM. I am writing a book about wife-swappers.

NANCY. Wife-swappers?

WILLIAM. Yes.
Wife-swappers on the Manchester, Altrincham and South
Junction Railway.

NANCY (*to mike*). I went down to the shed at the bottom of
the garden.
At least one thing would be normal.
At least I'd find Father tippling at his gin.
I burst open the door and he looked at me and said:

24

FATHER. Whato, Nancy.
Do you know I have never felt better in the whole of my life.

NANCY. What?

FATHER. I feel wonderful.

NANCY. But what about your legs?
What about your chest and your sinus and your attacks
of vertigo?

FATHER. All sound as a bell, Nancy.
And do you know what the reason is?

NANCY. Tell me.

FATHER. Living here.
In this village.
In this house.
Being part of the community.
Being part of the human race and feeling that I'm giving to my
fellow men without restraint the love and kindness and radiant
warmth that I've concealed all these years deep in my soul and . . .
And I've stopped drinking gin.

NANCY. Pardon?

FATHER. I don't think I ever told you, Nancy, but I've always been
a secret tippler.
I used to hide the bottles from you.
You never found out.
I was too clever.
I'm not pleased about it.
In fact I'm intensely ashamed about it.
But now it's all stopped, Nancy.
No more gin drinking for me.
I'm so happy.
Yes.
So happy.
I remember we used to drink rather a lot in India.
Gin.
Your mother and I.
Good God, oodles and oodles of gin.

NANCY (*almost screaming*). Father, Father, how can you?
How can you do this to me?
I can't cope with it.
I can't cope.
(*To mike:*) I fled back from the garden.
I raced upstairs.
I charged into my bedroom.

I flung myself on to my bed and I started to cry.
I hadn't cried like that since I was a little girl.
I used to cry a lot when I was a little girl when I couldn't cope.
And then I learned how to cope, and I didn't cry any more.
I cried, and I cried, and I cried.

25

The sound of the door opening.

WINSTON. Oh, not disturbing you, am I, missus?
    I just wanted to look at your . . .
    You're crying.

NANCY. Go away.

WINSTON. You're crying, Nancy.
    Why are you crying?

NANCY. I'm not crying.
    Go away.

WINSTON. Right then, I'll . . .

NANCY. No.
    Stay.

WINSTON. Right.
    I'll stay.
    I'd lend you my hankie only it's covered in snot see.
    Pause.
    Why was you crying, Nancy?

NANCY. I don't know.
    I just can't help it.

WINSTON. You didn't ought to cry at your age, missus.

NANCY. I'm not old.

WINSTON. I knows you're not old.
    You ain't old at all, missus.
    In fact, I think you look very young.
    You look very desirable if you don't mind me saying so.

NANCY. What?

WINSTON. You looks desirable.
    I'm an expert on women being desirable.
    Always have been all my life.
    That's how I knows my wife ain't desirable.
    That she ain't.
    Very far from it.

But you are.
Yes, you are, missus.
Very desirable indeed.

Pause.

You don't want a new downpipe for your outside bog, do you?
Free and gratis.

NANCY. Get out.
Get out, you disgusting man.
How dare you burst into my bedroom with your muddy boots and
your bad breath and your dirty hair.
Get out.
Out, out, out.

She begins to sob as the door slams shut.

26

NANCY (*to mike*). And minute by minute the days to the village fête
ticked by.
And minute by minute the feeling that I was being watched grew
stronger and stronger.
It made me shiver on the hottest of days.
It made me perspire at dusk when the chill breeze whipped the
surface of the chalk stream.
I could not sleep at night.
In the days my legs felt like lead and the pulses at my temples
twitched and throbbed.
And I was watching, too.
I was lurking in the shadows and watching them.
Him naked to the waist, hairy belly dusty and taut, smiling and
whistling through the gap in his two front teeth.
William laughing and quite blatantly going in and out of
Mrs Godwin's house.
Rosie laughing and going out in the car of an evening with
Winston in his corduroy suit and his pink shirt.
And one night he wore a different-coloured shirt.
It was pink with . . .
I saw Father smiling, too.
In his shed.
Not drinking.
Happy.
Not complaining about his health.
And all the time I knew there was someone watching me, too.
Then one night as I lay in bed on the Friday before the village
fête I realised what it was.
It was Wilson Rappaport.

It had to be.
He was still in this house.
He was looking at me from every nook and cranny like the spider
in the house we left in London.
And everything in the house was his.
Every person in the house was his.
He had taken them over.
Rosie's laughter was his.
Father's happiness was his.
William's ardour was his.
He had taken over every person in the house.
Everyone except me.
My little carriage clock ticked.
And it tocked.
I heard owls hooting and the scream of rabbits.
I heard the snuffle and squeak of mice and the scutter of starlings
in the eaves.
And I heard a floorboard creak outside my room.
And someone came into the room.
The door did not open, but I knew for certain that someone was
in the room.
It was a man.
I knew it was a man.
I could hear the rasp of his breath.
I stiffened in bed. I tensed up, I couldn't move.
The footsteps came nearer and nearer to me.
And it was as though the bedclothes were pulled off me, for
I suddenly felt cold.
I was rigid with terror.
I felt breath on my cheeks. And I felt hands on my body. I felt
hands running over my shoulders and over my breasts. And
I swear I had heard a voice say:
'Lucy.'
'Lucy, Lucy, it's me.'
I screamed.
I screamed at the top of my voice.
I leapt out of bed. I burst open the door. And I don't know why
I did it, but I ran downstairs, I ran through the kitchen, I ran
down the garden path to the shed. I burst open the door.
And there was William.
He was lying on the floor.
On his back.
Completely motionless.
And I screamed:
William, William, William.
Next thing I remember Rosie and Father were standing by
my side.
(*To* FATHER:) He's dead.

FATHER. He's not dead.
    He's drunk.

ROSIE. William?
    Drunk?

NANCY. He's dead.
    He's dead, I tell you.

FATHER. He's drunk.
    He's drunk as a lord.
    I've seen lots of drunks in my time.
    Saw loads of drunks in India.
    That's why we lost the Empire – drank it to death.
    Look at him.
    He's still breathing.
    Smell his breath.
    Whisky.
    He's been drinking gallons of the stuff.
    I'll give him a good kick in the ribs.
    That'll sort him out.
    There.
    Take that.

He kicks him in the ribs.

WILLIAM (*groans and cries out in pain*). Oh, Lucy.
    Lucy, Lucy.

NANCY. Lucy?
    What's Lucy got to do with it?

WILLIAM. She's abandoned me.
    She's thrown me to the wolves.
    Oh, Lucy, Lucy.

NANCY (*to mike*). We carried him into the house, undressed him and put him to bed.
    Next morning the day of the village fête he appeared at breakfast, and he was well-groomed and smart, and he was smiling.

27

ROSIE. You're smiling, William.

WILLIAM. Of course I'm smiling.
    Why shouldn't I smile?

ROSIE. But Mrs Godwin?
    I thought she'd abandoned you.

WILLIAM. Oh there are plenty more fish in the sea, Rosie.
Have you seen that Betty Hayball?
Cor.

NANCY (*softly to mike*). I can't cope.
I can't cope.

ROSIE. It's going to be a lovely, lovely day.
It's going to be one of the best days of my life.
A whole day at the stall with Winston.

NANCY (*to mike*). I couldn't help it.
I suddenly burst out:
(*To* ROSIE:) Winston!
Winston!
Why you have to go round with that slob I just do not know.
That disgusting man with his long greasy hair and his tattoos over
his nipples and his dirty, slimy teeth and his . . .

ROSIE. He is not a disgusting man.
He is not a slob.
Winston is one of the finest men I've ever met. He is a lovely,
lovely man, and if he weren't married, I would scoop him up and
we would run off and we would live in a caravan high in the hills
and we would go wandering round leafy lanes and our life would
be bliss and I'm not going to have you spoil my dreams.
You've spoiled our lives before with your bossing and your
martyrdom and your coping. Your constant bloody coping. And
I am not going to stand for it any longer.
Goodbye.

NANCY (*to mike*). And she marched out.
But she had a spring to her step.
And William ran off after her, and he, too, had a spring in
his step.
(*Softly:*) I can't cope. I can't cope.

FATHER. Yes.
Think I'll potter off, too.
Might just call in to the pub.
Just for a quick one.
Nothing alcoholic, of course.
A bloody Mary without the tomato juice.

28

NANCY (*to mike*). And he went, too.
I was on my own.
I was alone in that house.

But I was not being watched.
There was no one there.
And I couldn't cope.
I could not cope.
But I felt relaxed.
I felt at ease with the world.
How strange. How curious.
I put on my coat and I walked out of the front door.
I went down the little lane, turned right past the farmhouse, past the pub, and there was the meadow and there was the village fête.

A brass band.

I pressed myself into the old holly hedge and watched them.
The villagers enjoying themselves, letting themselves go, joining in.
Laughing and smiling.
And I couldn't laugh, and I couldn't smile.
But I wanted to.
I wanted to.
And there was Rosie laughing and smiling.
And there was William laughing and smiling.
And there was Father laughing and smiling.
And there was . . .

WINSTON. Hello, Nancy.

NANCY (*cries out with alarm*). Winston.
You gave me a start.

WINSTON. Yes.

Pause.

You looks unhappy.

NANCY. Me?

WINSTON. Yes.
You, Nancy.

NANCY (*pauses, then sharply*). Why aren't you at your stall?
You're supposed to be working with Rosie, aren't you?

WINSTON. I just slipped out for a couple of pints or two.
You want to come?

NANCY. To the pub?

WINSTON. No, not the village pub.
I'll take you to another pub look.
The pub I always takes my bits of fluff to.

NANCY. What?

WINSTON. Come on, missus.
Get in my car. Get in my motor.

I'll take you out.
I'll show you something nice.

29

NANCY (*to mike*). And to my amazement I got into his car.
I got into his motor.

WINSTON. Don't bother your head about seat belts.
I don't like bits of fluff wearing seat belts.
Hampers their mobility look.
Come on then.
Off we go.

The sound of the motor car.

NANCY (*to mike*). He didn't take me to the pub.
He took me to his house.

WINSTON. No need to look alarmed, Nancy.
The missus ain't in.
She's down at the fête.
She's on a stall look.
They throws wooden balls and if they hits the target, the missus
falls into a trough of cold water.
Talk about laugh.
Everyone laughs when an ugly woman falls in a trough of water.
It's one of the laws of the nature look.
I told you I was a philosopher.
Come on.
I'll show you my wood.

30

NANCY (*to mike*). And he took hold of my hand.
He squeezed it.
He took me into the wood.
There were birds singing.
And gently he took hold of my shoulders and sat me down at the
foot of a great beech tree.
He sat down beside me.

WINSTON. You ain't never had a man before, has you, Nancy?

NANCY. I . . . I . . .

WINSTON. You ain't never had a bloke in the whole of your life,
has you?

NANCY. No.

WINSTON. Why not, Nancy?

NANCY. I . . . I've been too busy keeping the family together.
I haven't had time.
All my life has been consumed by keeping them together.

WINSTON. Very noble, Nancy.
It's very noble to keep people together.
To pull them together.
To snuggle them up close together.

NANCY (*to mike*). And he pressed himself close into me.
I felt his breath on my cheek.
I felt his hands on my shoulders.
And they closed softly over my breasts.
And I said:
(*To* WINSTON:) Winston.
Winston, Winston.
(*To mike:*) And he said:

WINSTON. Nancy.
Nancy, Nancy.
This is the best village fête I ever been to since I was born.
That it is.
That it is, Nancy.

NANCY (*to mike*). Next morning Winston arrived early.
He smiled. He winked. And he said:

WINSTON. Hello, missus.
I got a present for you.

NANCY. What is it?

WINSTON. A new downpipe for your outside bogs.
Free and gratis.
Free and gratis.

NANCY (*to mike*). And he kissed me full on the lips.
And I hugged him tight to me.
And I shouted at the top of my voice:
(*To the garden:*) I'm happy.
I'm happy, I'm happy.